The Merrill Studies
in
Cane

Compiled by
Frank Durham
University of South Carolina

Charles E. Merrill Publishing Company
A Bell & Howell Company
Columbus, Ohio

CHARLES E. MERRILL STUDIES

Under the General Editorship of
Matthew J. Bruccoli and Joseph Katz

ISBN: 0–675–09202–7

Library of Congress Catalog Number: 76–151652

1 2 3 4 5 6 7 8 9 — 79 78 77 76 75 74 73 72 71

Printed in the United States of America

Preface

When Jean Toomer's *Cane* was published in 1923, it was noticed by only a very few reviewers and critics, most of them black, and it sold around five hundred copies. It seemed that, as Thomas Bailey Aldrich said of an early volume of Emily Dickinson's poems, "Oblivion lingers in the immediate neighborhood." It is now known that Toomer continued to write, but after *Cane* he published only a few pieces in "little" magazines, a play *Balo* (1927), and a privately printed collection of epigrams and aphorisms called *Essentials* (*ca.* 1932). The rest was silence—and mystery. To all intents and purposes, Jean Toomer vanished. In efforts to see him, people like Allen Tate made appointments for meetings, but when the time came Toomer failed to appear. Occasionally, the cloud of obscurity lifted slightly as when he refused to allow his poems and stories to be reprinted in collections of black literature and cryptically proclaimed that neither he nor his writings were Negro. His marriage to Margery Latimer caused a minor and brief sensation, and there was a slight stir when it was discovered that his daughter was a student in a fashionable Quaker school. On the few occasions that he was forced to relinquish momentarily his chosen oblivion, he was quoted as denying that he was a member of the Negro race and affirming instead that he was an "American." At his death in 1967 he was apparently almost forgotten, and his masterwork had been out of print for nearly half a century.

However, as a matter of fact, a few did not forget him. *Cane*, in spite of (perhaps because of) all its strangeness, lingered in the memories of a handful of critics, both black and white. From time to time, mainly in journals devoted to black culture, someone wrote about *Cane* and Toomer, often trying to penetrate the mystery of why he had so abruptly turned his back on what seemed a significant career in American letters. Generally favorable reassessments of *Cane* also appeared and there were pleas that the book be reprinted and made available to a new generation of readers, one which has become increasingly appreciative of the contribution of black culture to American literature.

Finally, in 1969, two years after Toomer's death, Harper and Row brought out a new paperback edition of *Cane* in their Perennial Classic series. It found a receptive audience among both scholars and general readers, and already stories and poems by Toomer, often from *Cane* itself, are being included in anthologies of American literature.

The story of Jean Toomer and *Cane*, then, follows the archetypal pattern of birth, death, and resurrection, on a smaller scale perhaps, but similar to the stories of the reputations of Herman Melville, Henry James, F. Scott Fitzgerald, and other American writers who have experienced oblivion and rehabilitation.

One of the purposes of the present volume is to bring together the documents which will enable the reader to trace the history of *Cane*'s literary reputation. The first section presents an excerpt from Mabel M. Dillard's unpublished doctoral dissertation which is, at present, the only full-length study of Toomer. Included in this excerpt are several letters and statements by Toomer himself, directed generally to such literary friends and associates as Sherwood Anderson and Waldo Frank. In these letters Toomer defines his esthetic as well as his desire to present the Negro race spiritually and to capture its essence before this essence is corrupted by the dominant white society. But even in these letters and statements of belief come foreshadowings of the later denials of race which so upset Toomer's admirers, especially those who had hailed him as the portrayer of the soul of the Negro. The other two brief pieces in this first section—my own and a story from *Time*—show incidents in Toomer's biography which cast some light on both his attitude toward the society in which he found himself and the attitude of that society, especially its Southern segment, toward him.

In the second section I have reprinted the introductions to the two editions of *Cane*. The first, for the 1923 edition, presents Toomer's friend Waldo Frank making an impassioned and almost lyrical plea that the book be judged, not as a Negro book, not as a book concerned with race, but as a work of art. From one point of view, Frank is prophetic of the paradox of Toomer's career, for Toomer was apparently so determined to be evaluated purely as an artist that he turned away from the subject of the Negro, the vital source of his peculiar art, and lost himself in rather abstruse philosophical studies. The results of this rejection, now on deposit at Fisk University Library, are several unpublished novels by Jean Toomer, novels about white people.

If Frank's introduction has the tone of hopeful beginnings, that of Arna Bontemps in 1969 sounds a kind of requiem for a great talent misused and lost. What Bontemps does is to engage in an investigation of the why of Jean Toomer's failure to move forward from " 'the most astonishingly brilliant beginning of any Negro writer of this generation' " and from the creation of a work which strongly affected "practically an entire generation of young Negro writers then just beginning to emerge." He finds his answer in the biography of Toomer, a man suspended between two races and two cultures who never really found out who he was and whose talent atrophied in a world which drove him relentlessly in the search for his own identity. What Bontemps implies, of course, is that the tragedy of Jean Toomer is more than a uniquely personal one. It is too often the tragedy of the sensitive American Negro who is also an artist.

The contemporary reviews brought together in the third section of this book shed light, I believe, on the confusion with which *Cane* was greeted. In 1923 *Cane* was indisputably *sui generis.* Nobody quite knew what to make of it, for *Cane* consists of a mixture of poetry, poetic prose sketches, fairly straight short stories, and something that starts as fiction and then, seemingly, turns into a play. Its first section deals with Georgia Negroes, the second with the Southern Negro transplanted to the urban ghetto of Washington, D.C., and the third, once again set in Georgia, with a "foreign" Negro's difficulties there and his relation to the native Negroes. Was this book some new kind of novel? Was it an anthology? Did all its various parts blend into a subtle unity? Or was it, as one reviewer called it, merely "A Literary Vaudeville"? The confusion of white reviewers is obvious. John Armstrong of the *New York Tribune* hailed *Cane* as evidence of the Southern Negro's at last finding "an authentic lyric voice," yet complained that the book is sometimes "strident" and "inarticulately maudlin"; he praised Toomer's authentic portrait of the Negro but described the book as "a volume of short stories." Bruno Lasker called *Cane* "fragmentary," a "medley," and even denied the existence of its nominal author. He was convinced that the book was an unpolished exercise by Waldo Frank. The anonymous critic of the *Boston Transcript* was almost totally at a loss, wavering among holding the lyrical style up for ridicule, calling *Cane* "a curious concoction," and praising its fresh portrayal of the Negro. Robert Littell mingled his objections to the more staccato rhythms of the style (like "Western Union") with praise for Toomer's work as poetry and an "exploration" of "new ways of writing."

The black reviewers seemed surer of what they were reading and generally recognized *Cane* as a significant evidence that the black writer was coming into his own as an artist and as an experimenter in form and language, free from restrictive impulses toward propaganda and protest. Montgomery Gregory saw *Cane* as a fusion of verse, fiction, and drama "into a spiritual unity, an 'aesthetic equivalent' of the Southland." Its meaning was not to be understood from a literal reading; "it must be emotionally, aesthetically felt." W. E. B. DuBois, too, stressed the importance of *Cane* as art and of Toomer as a Negro writer of great promise. Particularly, he was pleased that Toomer was the first black writer to dare "to emancipate the colored world from the conventions of sex," and he hoped for much more from Toomer in the future. Robert T. Kerlin, on the other hand, seemed to share some of the confusion of the white reviewers, for he included *Cane* in an omnibus review of three volumes of poetry by Negro poets.

The fourth and final section comprises longer critical essays on Toomer and *Cane* by black and white critics dating from 1925 to 1969. For though the book quickly vanished from the bookshops, every decade since its publication found somebody inspired to write about it and its author. Somehow *Cane* would not join that roomy limbo which houses so many hopeful efforts of the past. The persistent interest of the black critics is understandable, for *Cane* did indeed represent the first effort by a Negro writer to use language as an art form in itself, and it did present a unique portrait of the Negro in terms of his spirit rather than in terms of his comic or touching or militant stereotypes. Then, too, the enigma of Toomer tantalized the black critics, just as it was to tantalize the white ones. Was there something to be learned from him about the difficulties of the Negro artist in a white-dominated society and culture? Again and again, these black critics trace and retrace the known facts of Toomer's life in their search for an answer. Eugene Holmes repeats the earlier pronouncement that Toomer was the first Negro to write as a poet and an artist and not as "a Negro poet," but also stresses his influence on Negro poets who followed him. Saunders Redding also emphasizes the significance of Toomer's experimentation and of his influence on subsequent Negro writing. A similar stance is taken by Hugh M. Gloster in his brief analysis of *Cane* when he points out the influence upon Toomer of his white friends Sherwood Anderson and Waldo Frank. I have quoted little more than a paragraph from Alain Locke's 1953 article simply to show that thirty years after its publication *Cane* was listed by a distinguished Negro critic as the first of the "three points of peak development in Negro fiction by Negro writers" during the three decades, the other two being Richard Wright's *Native Son* and Ralph Ellison's *Invisible Man*. In their essays, Robert A. Bone, S. P. Fullenwider, and Arna Bontemps go beyond an analysis of Toomer and his work as art into an attempt to place him in the context of the Harlem Writers and the Negro Renaissance of the 1920's. Darwin T. Turner's essay considers Toomer's dramatic writings, including *Kabis* from *Cane*, and attributes their failure to gain an audience to the fact that, amid the American dramatic experimentation of the late teens and early twenties, Toomer's work foreshadowed the Theatre of the Absurd and was thus ahead of its time.

The white critics are represented by two friends and associates of Toomer who were writing shortly after the publication of *Cane;* by David Littlejohn, who attempts an objective analysis of Toomer and *Cane* free both from the bonds of friendship and from the preoccupations of earlier critics; and by the present writer, who relates Toomer's portrayal of the Negro to the Harlem School and more recent black writings and who suggests that Toomer's work was not as free of protest against the oppression of the Negro as it has been usual to say.

Both Rosenfeld and Munson were in a position to know Toomer's intentions, but they belonged to his circle and neither fully avoided the temptation to "puff" a friend's work. Rosenfeld stresses the influence of Sherwood Anderson, Waldo Frank, the Imagists, and, in passing, James Joyce. Again we hear of Toomer the artist, the capturer of the Negro's soul, without prejudice, propaganda, or protest. At first, emphasis in Munson's essay is also on Toomer the stylist whose words were indebted to his love of music; but he moves on to praise of Toomer the philosopher, the seeker of answers to great questions. He finds Toomer turning inward to a study of his own psychology in the search for these answers, a search that is not ended and may, in fact, be endless. And here, unconsciously, Munson foreshadows the causes of Toomer's disastrous plunge from literature into the mazes of mysticism, psychologizing and philosophizing. In his brief discussion of Jean Toomer, David Littlejohn is concerned with assessing him mainly as a poet and stylist, considering him with Countee Cullen, Claude McKay, and Langston Hughes as the chief Negro poets to emerge in the 1920's. He sees Toomer as a sophisticate, an alien, viewing both the Southern and the urban Negro through the distorting mirror of the "Stein-Hemingway-Anderson tradition" abetted by a kind of surrealistic symbolism. Of recent critics, he seems to have the most reservations about the value of Toomer as an artist whose work will be remembered. My own essay affirms the oft-noted skill with which Toomer depicts the Southern Negro's soul, his closeness to the life-giving Georgia earth and his ties with his African origins. Further, it maintains—other interpreters to the contrary—that implicit in his picture of the Negro's relationship to white culture and white dominance, there is a strong but subtle protest at the injustice and violence to which the black man is subjected, a protest all the more persuasive because it is organic to his vision of the Negro and is not shrill and blatant like that of the overt propagandist.

Cane will, in its new life, be of especial interest to the students of black culture. First, it is a literary presentation by a Negro of the Negro's spirit, of what Mabel Dillard calls "soul." And it antedates contemporary attempts in this area by close to half a century. It came at a time when white Southern writers were just discovering the black man as a subject for literature—Clement Wood's *Nigger* (1922), T. S. Stribling's *Birthright* (1922), DuBose Heyward's *Porgy* (1925), and Julia Peterkin's *Green Thursday* (1924). With the emerging propagandistic school represented by the first two works, *Cane* had little in common; in its use of the primitive Negro as a subject for a compassionate art, it is closer to the work of Mrs. Peterkin and Heyward (who, Toomer said, influenced him), but it is markedly different from them in style and concepts of form. His work, in some ways, is rightly classed with that of the Harlem School of the Negro Renaissance in its efforts, devoid of propaganda, to stress the Negro's "Negritude" and to show him suspended between two cultures and drawing from the African one a vitality and *panache* denied the white man. Yet *Cane* will not remain fixed in either of these categories. For, though he was hailed by black reviewers and influenced black writers, Toomer himself really learned his craft and found his intellectual and spiritual milieu among the circle of white writers and artists made up of Sherwood Anderson, Hart Crane, Waldo Frank, Paul Rosenfeld, Gorham Munson, Georgia O'Keefe, and Alfred Stieglitz. With them he shared a dedication to writing as an art, not a Negro art, not really a humanist art, but one which stressed style and form and symbol and perception. He was an early American exemplar of a kind of international art for art's sake mystique which is not unrelated to the theories and practice of Joyce and others from across the Atlantic; he was undoubtedly the first Negro writer to venture into this field, and it is no wonder that, from the first, black reviewers and later black essayists, in spite of the smallness of his output and his denials of his Negritude, pointed to him with pride as the first Negro stylist and artist.

In searching for some of the essays included in this book I received invaluable assistance from Dr. Harriet Holman of Clemson University and my son Frank Durham, Jr. I wish to thank Mrs. Frances Perry for clerical assistance.

FD

Contents

4. Critical Essays

A. Black Critics

B. White Critics

1. Toomer's Esthetic Ideas and Fragments of His Biography

Mabel Mayle Dillard

Behind the Veil:
Jean Toomer's Esthetic

... Toomer felt that he himself had a natural and a real proclivity for knowing wherein lay the beauty of the Negro race. This knowledge, he said, became fully apparent to him after he had read [Sherwood] Anderson's work and [Waldo] Frank's *Rehab* and *Dark Mother*. Toomer told Frank in a letter:

> Sherwood Anderson has doubtless a very deep and beautiful emotion by way of the Negro. Here and there he has succeeded in expressing this. But he is not satisfied. He wants more. He is hungry for it. I come along. I express it. It is natural for him to see me in terms of this expression. I see myself that way. But also I see myself expressing myself, expressing *Life*. I expect artists to recognize the circle of expression. When they don't, I'm not disappointed; I simply know that in this respect they differ but little from the mass which must narrow and caricature if it is to grasp the thing at all. Sherwood's notes are very deep and sincere. Hence I attribute his attitude to a natural limitation. This limitation, extended, is noticeable in the bulk of his work. The range of his sensibility, curiosity, and intelligence is not very wide. One's admiration suffers, but one's personal liking need not be affected by this.
>
> There is one thing about the Negro in America which most thoughtful persons seem to ignore: the Negro is in solution, in the process of solution. As an entity, the race is losing its body, and its soul is approaching a common soul. If one holds his eyes to individuals and sections, race is starkly evident, and racial continuity seems assured. One is even led to believe that the thing we call Negro beauty will always be attributable to a clearly defined physical source. But the fact is, that if anything comes up now, pure Negro, it will be a swan song. Don't let us fool ourselves, brother: the Negro of the folk-song has all but passed away: the Negro of the emotional church is fading. A hundred years from now these Negroes, if they exist at all, will live in art. And I be-

Printed from "Jean Toomer: Herald of the Negro Renaissance" (Unpublished Doctoral Dissertation, Ohio University, 1967) pp. 18–30, by permission of the author. The editor thanks Mrs. Marjorie Content Toomer and Fisk University Library for permission to publish the excerpts from Jean Toomer's letters and manuscripts cited herein.

lieve that a vague sense of this fact is the driving force behind art movements directed toward him today. (Likewise the Indian.) American [sic] needs these elements. They are passing. Let us grab and hold this solution. But in the end, segregation will either give way, or it will kill. Natural preservations do not come from unnatural laws. The supreme fact of mechanical civilization is that you become a part of it, or get sloughed off (under). Negroes have no culture to resist it with (and if they had, their position would be identical to that of the Indians), hence industrialism the more readily transforms them. A few generations from now, the Negro will still be dark, and a portion of his psychology will spring from this fact, but in all else he will be a conformist to the general outlines of American civilization, or of American chaos. In my own stuff, in those pieces that come nearest to the old Negro, to the spirit saturate with folk-song: "Karintha" and "Fern," the dominant emotion is a sadness derived from a sense of fading, from a knowledge of my futility to check solution. There is nothing about these pieces of the buoyant expression of a new race. The folk-songs themselves are of the same order. The deepest of them. "I ain't got long to stay here." Religiously: "I (am going) to cross over into camp ground." Socially: "My position here is transient. I'm going to die or be absorbed." [1]

Toomer was aware that the literature of America had not properly depicted the role which the Negro had played in American civilization. He emphasized to Frank that the Negro was in the process "of solution" and that within a few years he would be dissolved into the culture of America, since he had no culture of his own to cling to. And Toomer wanted to capture these emotions of the "pure Negro" so that he might create art forms. He recognized that the sudden interest of the Negro Renaissance in Negro literature, art, and music was an important movement, but that no American author had ever caught these emotions of the Negro. He realized that the literature of America ought to include these materials before the American Negro had completely conformed to the "general outlines of American civilization and chaos."

But the city of Washington, he told Frank, though it provided him with "crude materials," left him literally starved and he began to feel an urge to know the other areas of America, especially those areas where the Negro population was more dense as well as more primitive. He and Frank, who was also writing literature about

---

[1] Extract from an undated letter from Jean Toomer to Waldo Frank (*ca.* 1922), Toomer Collection, Fisk University Library.

Negroes, planned a trip south, to the South that was "unspoiled" by integration, miscegenation, and mechanization, where they might observe Negroes more closely. To become acquainted with these Negroes, Toomer and Frank decided to go to a Southern area where they might associate with these Americans who lived close to the soil. They went to rural Georgia. Before he left Washington with Frank, Toomer had told him:

> At whatever town we stay, I'll have to be known as a Negro. First, only because by experiencing white pressure can the venture bear its fullest fruit. Second, because the color of my skin (it is nearly black from the sun) at the present time makes such a course a physical necessity. This, however, will not hinder our intercourse. Should make the exchange more complete, in fact.[2]

This trip to Georgia provided Toomer, and Frank as well [,] with material that helped the two of them to discover America. In his *The Re-Discovery of America*, Frank has attributed his real knowledge of America to the materials he found while on his trip with Toomer:

> Then, America came to my weariness: the America of beauty and splendour.... The Negro South, where with my friend Jean Toomer I had lived within the veil, drinking the warm life that rises and blows within the cane and the other South, bled white, maimed of limb, palsied of head, the stiff-eyed, loveable childish South of the masters.[3]

Toomer's extensive reading had convinced him that the spirit of the Negro had not been satisfactorily expressed, an opinion borne out by what he discovered among the Negroes of Georgia. Having observed that many Negroes were a "diluted" form of the race, he made another trip, this time to Harper's Ferry, West Virginia, where he had hoped to obtain other valuable insights into the Negro race. This trip, however, was a disappointment to him. He told Waldo Frank:

> Life here has not the vividity and distinction of that of Middle Georgia. Racial attitudes, on both sides, are ever so much more tolerant, even friendly. Oppression and ugly emotions seem

---

[2] Extract from a letter from Jean Toomer to Waldo Frank, dated August 15, 1921, Waldo Frank Collection, University of Pennsylvania Library.
[3] Waldo Frank, *The Re-Discovery of America* (New York, 1929), p. 3.

nowhere in evidence. And there are no folk songs. A more stringent grip, I guess, is necessary to force them through. But Southern life is surely here. Stringy, ruddy whites, worn; full blooded blacks, and I think I see a strain of Indian blood. Localism is somewhat diluted by the influx of transients.[4]

In contrast to the "pseudo-urbanized" Negroes of Washington and New York and to the "diluted" Negroes that he found in Harper's Ferry, Toomer had found in the rural South the sources that he had long sought for in his artistic expression. In a letter to Lola Ridge, he had observed some time after this trip:

The South needs consciousness and pruning. And the courage to break through the New England to itself. Abundance, there is. But those who are most capable of using it are invariably the most inhibited. This for the whites. More so for the blacks. It would surprise you to see the anemia and timidity (emotional) in folk but a generation or so removed from the Negroes of the folk-songs. Full blooded people to look at who are afraid to hold hands, much less to love.[5]

Toomer believed that the literature of America ought to include the artistic expression of the "truth of the South" before such a time in the future when the "Negro of the folk-song" and of the "emotional church" had died completely away. The trip which Toomer made to Georgia gave him what he had been searching for to fulfill his "growing need for artistic expression." He summarized, in his autobiography, the results of the trip:

There, for the first time, I really saw the Negro, not as a pseudo-urbanized and vulgarized, a semi-Americanized product, but the Negro peasant, strong with the tang of fields and the soil. It was there that I first heard folk-songs rolling up the valley at twilight, heard them as spontaneous with gold, and tints of an eternal purple. Love? They gave birth to a whole new life.[6]

Toomer hoped that his artistic expression about Negroes would set new literary standards for Negro writers. He already knew that

---

[4] Extract from a letter from Jean Toomer to Waldo Frank, dated August, 1922, Toomer Collection, Fisk University Library.

[5] Extract from a letter from Jean Toomer to Lola Ridge, dated August 20, 1922, Toomer Collection, Fisk University Library.

[6] Jean Toomer, "Outline of Autobiography" (Unpublished MS., *ca.* 1934), Toomer Collection, Fisk University Library, p. 57.

the economic and professional struggles of Negroes prevented their predilection toward literary endeavors. Moreover, the stigma generally associated with being a Negro had caused them to deny their heritage, whereas Toomer, whose family had once been what are called "good livers," was eager to delve into the folk ways of the Negro and to relate this heritage to the cultural development of the entire United States. "No picture of a Southern person is complete without its bit of Negro-determined psychology," he told Waldo Frank in commenting on the latter's book, *Our America.*[7]

Early in his writing career, he had endeavored to develop his talent for recording the lives of Negroes. Sherwood Anderson, for one, had believed that Toomer had a great talent for "writing Negro." For several years, then, Toomer had concentrated his efforts solely on developing his art of "writing Negro," that is writing about Negroes who had not denied their racial heritage nor sought approximation of Anglo-Saxon ideals.

He wrote Frank concerning his convictions about his literary intentions:

> Within the last two or three years, however, my growing need for artistic expression has pulled me deeper and deeper into the Negro group. And as my powers of receptivity increased, I found myself loving in a way I could never love the other. It has stimulated and fertilized whatever creative talent I may contain within me. The visit to Georgia last fall was the starting point of almost everything of worth that I have done. I heard folk-songs come from the lips of Negro peasants. I saw the rich dusk beauty that I heard many false accounts about, and of which, till then, I was somewhat skeptical. And a deep part of my nature, a part that I had repressed, sprang suddenly into life and responded to them. Now I can conceive of myself as aloof and separated. My point of view has not changed; it has deepened; it has widened. Personally, my life has been tenuous and dispersed. . . . Neither the universities of Wisconsin or New York gave me what I wanted, so I quit them. Just how I finally found my stride in writing, is difficult to lay hold of.[8]

Toomer, after he had lived close to Negroes in Georgia for a few months, began to write. His sketches and poems appeared in the

---

[7] Extract from a letter from Jean Toomer to Waldo Frank, dated March 24, 1922, Toomer Collection, Fisk University Library.
[8] Toomer, "Outline of Autobiography," p. 55.

small literary magazines in rapid succession: "Karintha" and "Kabnis" (the dramatic version) in *Broom;* three poems, "Storm Ending," "Harvest Song," and "Nora" in *Double Dealer;* "Song of the Sun" [sic] in *Crisis;* and "Fern" in *The Little Review.* Spurred on by the ready acceptance of his work and by editors' requests that he submit materials, as well as by the favorable criticism that he had received from critics and authors like Frank, Anderson, and John McClure of *Double Dealer,* Toomer devoted his literary talents to depicting the Negro of the cane- and cotton-fields. And with this work, his artistic powers reached their greatest intensity.

Toomer, in his personal life, mingled freely with Negroes and then circled out to include literary artists who shared his interests. For awhile, he associated with the Negro intellectuals in Harlem during the Negro Renaissance: Arna Bontemps, Claude McKay, the painter Aaron Douglass, Langston Hughes, Countee Cullen, Jessie Fauset, and Zora Neale Hurston. "He was as Negro as any of us then," recalled Mr. Douglass when asked about Toomer's activities in Harlem.[9] These Negro litterateurs, who were at that time achieving their maturity (during the Negro Renaissance), also recognized that Toomer had surpassed most of them in the artistry of his work. Claude Barnett, of the Associated Negro Press, when he first saw the work of Toomer, felt that Toomer could not write as he did unless he was a Negro, but his white literary friends would not concede that Toomer's style and the polish of his work were Negroid. The prevailing opinion of literary America toward Negroes at that time may be seen by the following letter from Claude Barnett to Toomer:

Dear Mr. Toomer:

For sometime we, and by we I mean a group of three friends, the other two whom are literary men, one colored and one white, have wondered who and what you are. There have been several arguments, the literary men contending that your style and finish are not Negroid, while I, who am but the business manager of a news service, felt certain that you were—for how else could you interpret "us" as you do unless you had peeked behind the veil?

We would welcome an opportunity to publish anything which you felt would be suitable for these weekly papers which we serve. Good fiction they have never had. The field is really ripe and I

---

[9] Statement made to the writer by Mr. Aaron Douglass at Nashville, Tennessee, February 17, 1967.

believe much worthwhile effort and literary interest would be stimulated by your appearance in these papers.[10]

To which Toomer promptly replied:

Dear Mr. Barnett:

The arguments you have had with your friends, the different points of view and the consequent contentions, are not at all peculiar to your group. . . . The true and complete answer is one of some complexity, and for this reason perhaps it will not be seen and accepted until after I am dead. The answer involves a realistic and accurate knowledge of racial mixture, of nationality as formed by the interaction of tradition, culture, and environment, of the artistic nature of its relation to the racial or social group, etc. All of which, of course, is too heavy and thick to go into now. Let me state then, simply, that I am the grandson of the late P. B. S. Pinchback. From this fact, it is clear that your contention is sustained. I have "peeped behind the veil." And my deepest impulse to literature (on the side of material) is the direct result of what I saw. In so far as the old folk-songs, syncopated rhythms, the rich sweet taste of dark-skinned life, in so far as these are Negro, I am, body and soul, Negroid. My style, my esthetic, is nothing more nor less than my attempt to fashion my substance into works of art. For it, I am indebted to my inherent gifts, and to the entire body of contemporary literature. I see no reason why my style and finish could not have come from an American with Negro blood in his veins. The pure fact is that they have so come, and hence your friends' contentions are thrown out of court. . . .

My aim is to direct the people's sensitivity and perception to the beauty that is at hand, and, if I am particularly fortunate, to stimulate someone to an expression of his immediate life.[11]

Toomer felt that his "flesh and blood and spirit" were struggling to give birth to creation, and he continually hoped that he would be able to create something about Negroes that would be "in a small measure beautiful."

[In the remainder of this paragraph, which is here omitted, Dr. Dillard quotes comments on Toomer made by W. E. B. DuBois (though she attributes DuBois' comment to Alain Locke) in "The

---

[10] Extract from a letter from Claude Barnett to Jean Toomer, dated April 23, 1923, Toomer Collection, Fisk University Library.
[11] Extract from a letter from Jean Toomer to Claude Barnett, dated April 29, 1923, Toomer Collection, Fisk University Library.

Younger Literary Movement," *Crisis*, XXVII (February, 1924), 162, and by William Stanley Braithwaite, "The Negro in Literature," *Crisis*, XXVIII (September, 1924), 207. The DuBois article is reprinted in full in this volume, and the Braithwaite critique appears also in Arna Bontemps' "The Negro Renaissance: Jean Toomer and the Harlem Writers," reprinted in this collection.]

It is not to be implied that Jean Toomer was the only or the first American author who was attempting to advance the Negro as material for artistic treatment. Other American authors were recognizing that the Negro, as an integral part of American civilization, should serve as an excellent source for such treatment. But Jean Toomer was the first American of Negro heritage who recognized the possibility of so treating the Negro and who treated him with such emotion and such depth. He delved deeply into the Negro's psyche and tried to express his true feeling. In addition, he showed a more accurate depiction of the black world welling up against the white, in such a way that this social mingling had never been treated. J. Saunders Redding remarked in a resume of the influence on literature written by Negroes that the work of Jean Toomer was greatly influenced by Eugene O'Neill, Paul Rosenfeld, and DuBose Heyward. Redding outlined the two aspects of writing by Negroes at this time: the "arty, self-conscious and experimental" aspect of Jean Toomer and the other type which he characterized as "naïve and sophisticated, hysterical and placid, frivolous and sober, free and enslaved." [12] Evidences of the latter type may be seen in such works as James Weldon Johnson's *God's Trombones* and Claude McKay's *Banana Bottom*. This type attracted more readers. At the same time, Negro material was passing into the hands of writers who commercialized it. Carl Van Vechten's *Nigger Heaven* is such a work. During the Twenties, Harlem and its activities had become a fad for white America, both in its social activities and in literature and art. Most of the writers of this period just prior to the depression were concerned with advertising the gaiety of Harlem life or depicting its sordidness. That the Negro author was enthralled with the idea of delineating every phase of Negro life is borne out by even a rapid survey of the literature by Negro Renaissance (1920–1930) [writers], as well as the literature by Negro authors of the period preceding this one.

---

[12] J. Saunders Redding, "American Negro Literature," *The American Scholar*, XVIII (Spring, 1949), 137.

Much of the literature, one critic claimed, hoisted the "sewer to the people's noses." [13] But Jean Toomer had no desire to perpetuate the traditions common to Negro authors: the sensational or the primitivism.

In regard to the materials he was using for his work, he wrote to Claude McKay:

> From my own point of view, I am naturally and inevitably an American. I have striven for a spiritual fusion analagous to the fact of racial intermingling. Without denying a single element within me, with no desire to subdue, one to the other, I have sought to let them function as complements. I have tried to let them live in harmony.... Just how I came to find my stride in writing is difficult to lay hold of. It has been pushing through me for the last four years. For two years now, I have been in solitude here in Washington. I may be begging hunger to say that I am staking my living on my work. So be it. The mould is cast, and I cannot turn my back now even if I would.[14]

Thus, Jean Toomer broke away from the traditions of literature about Negroes. Inasmuch as his major concern was with literature as art, he did not cater to the demands of his reading public by treating the Negro as a stereotype. He treated Negroes who were full of vitality and emotion, not the dice-shooting, chicken-stealing Negroes, but those who had genuine poetic feelings. For Toomer to make this break with the literary traditions in writing about Negroes required stringent demands of his own creative powers as well as of his reading public. Nevertheless, he looked beyond the usual methods of the conventional treatment of Negroes, delved into the study of psychology and philosophy, and sought thereby to improve his literary style.

---

[13] George W. Jacobs, "Negro Authors Must Eat," *The Nation,* CXXVIII (June 12, 1949), 711.
[14] Extract from a letter from Jean Toomer to Claude McKay, dated August 19, 1922, Toomer Collection, Fisk University Library.

Frank Durham

The Only Negro Member
of the Poetry Society
# of South Carolina

The year 1923 was a turbulent one for the Poetry Society of South Carolina. Founded in 1920 with high hopes, a membership of over two hundred, and a waiting list,[1] the Society began, in 1923, to experience the aches and pains leading to its actual, if unofficial, subsiding into innocuous desuetude around 1925.[2] Two of its founders, DuBose Heyward and Hervey Allen, were increasingly neglecting the Society for the advancement of their own careers, while the other founder, the older John Bennett, was left to handle the affairs of the organization on its home ground, Charleston, South Carolina.

Two of the major disturbances, from the vantage point of today, reflect both the parochial nature and the outmoded racial attitudes of a good many of the literary groups of the Southern Renascence. Today, when skepticism shocks only the most unworldly, it is hard to recapture the outrage evoked by an "atheistic" poem in the South in 1923. Today, when black is beautiful and most groups make mighty efforts to secure at least token black members, it is difficult to reconstruct imaginatively the horror felt by the founders of the Poetry Society of South Carolina in 1923 when they discovered that on their membership roll was the name of a gentleman of color and, adding insult to injury, that he was about to publish a volume nationally advertised as "a book about negroes by a negro." Additional irony comes from the fact that today, when most of the books by the founders and the early lights of the Society are out of print, the author of the questionable poem is

Reprinted from "The Poetry Society of South Carolina's Turbulent Year: Self-Interest, Atheism and Jean Toomer," in *Southern Humanities Review*, V (January, 1971), 41–45, by permission of the editors of the *Southern Humanities Review*.

[1] See my *DuBose Heyward: The Man Who Wrote Porgy* (Columbia, S.C.: University of South Carolina Press, 1954), pp. 24–25.
[2] For an account of the decline of the Society, see my "The Rise of DuBose Heyward and the Rise and Fall of the Poetry Society of South Carolina," *Mississippi Quarterly*, XIX (Spring, 1966), 66–78.

venerated and the "book about negroes by a negro" has been rediscovered, reprinted, and hailed as a significant work of American literature.

For the scandalous poet was John Crowe Ransom, and the Negro member of the Poetry Society of South Carolina was Jean Toomer, author of *Cane*.

[Next comes an account of jealousies within the Society and the rather stormy reaction to Ransom's poem "Armageddon" and its winning a major prize offered by the Society.]

The dust of this battle hardly settled before what undoubtedly seemed the major cataclysm of 1923 rose to distress the patient John Bennett, now busily engaged in reading the proofs for the [Society's] *Year Book*.

There were two types of membership in the Poetry Society of South Carolina, resident and non-resident. Resident members, usually Charlestonians, paid full dues and were on hand for the local meetings of the Society. Non-resident members, sight unseen by the organization, paid lower dues and received a subscription to the *Year Book*. At the back of each *Year Book* appeared the lists of both types of members. Also, each *Year Book* featured a column called "Activities of Members" in which were reported, among other things, the publications of both resident and non-resident members.

In the late summer of 1923, resting from his proofreading, Bennett turned for pleasure to the book review section of the *New York Times*. Suddenly an advertisement by the firm of Boni and Liveright caught his eye and stirred his memory. Apparently he was much upset by what he saw and had Mrs. Bennett clip the advertisement for enclosure with letters both she and he were to write Heyward.

Bennett's letter, dated August 19, referred to the "item" as something "which calls for handling." He continued:

> As she writes you, this JEAN TOOMER is a NON-RESIDENT MEMBER of the Poetry Society. The name stands on the list of our members for 1922–1923, about to be printed . . (or not printed . . God knows!), . . and among the responses to the questionaire [sic] letter sent our [for "out"] for information concerning activities of our members, stands a reply from JEAN TOOMER. Hence there is a paragraph among ACTIVITIES OF MEMBERS

referring to TOOMER. Also there is a NOTICE OF BOOK BY
MEMBER among those I sent you. Whether this individual joined
the Society with the deliberate intention of starting trouble for us
if ejected, or of causing a row by discovery that the Poetry Society
of South Carolina had a negro member, I do not know. I fear all
this may come out with the publication of this book in the Fall,
by BONI & LIVERIGHT. There must be reviews of the author
and book procured by B. & L., in papers seen by our members
resident and non-resident. There may possibly be inserted somewhere, in some paper unaware of the row, or delighted with it, the
fact that TOOMER, the author of "Cane," "a book about negroes
by a negro," is a MEMBER OF THE POETRY SOCIETY OF
SOUTH CAROLINA.

Now, what is to be done? Strike out the book-notice and ex-
punge the name from the list of members? Refuse further membership by stating that TOOMER obtained such on false pretenses?

There is a chance that even our good friend [William Stanley]
Braithwaite, of the many friendly anthologies [Mr. Braithwaite,
a Negro, included in his anthologies poems by Poetry Society
members.], might note the facts if the book comes under his eye
for review. I have been puzzling, and asking everywhere among
the Charleston folk I see, as to who this TOOMER may be . . .
but could get no information.

How to prevent more TOOMERS, and more BOOBS from becoming members of various sorts, requiring notice under
ACTIVITIES is another searching query.

I just chanced to notice this item concerning TOOMER in running over the TIMES. It is to laugh! Eh? Or not to laugh? [3]

[The capitalization and punctuation are those of the original.]

Poor Bennett, a kind and humane gentleman if ever there was
one, was also both a man of the late nineteenth century and an
Ohioan strongly converted to Southern ways of thought. Too, he
was the embattled official of a Poetry Society dependent for its
existence upon dues paid and support given by Southerners less
Reconstructed than most—old line Charlestonians. His anxiety is
understandable.

So far as can be determined, the Poetry Society nowhere in its
regulations stipulated that its membership was to be confined to
people of the Caucasian race. So Toomer had, technically, not obtained membership on false pretenses. But in Charleston in 1923

---

[3] Extract from letter is used with the permission of Mr. Bennett and Miss
Susan Bennett. The letter is on deposit at the South Carolina Historical
Society, Charleston, S.C.

the spirit of the law was based on an assumption held in common by most white people, regardless of what the letter of the law might be. To them no Negro was ever intended to be a member of the Poetry Society of South Carolina—who ever heard of a Negro poet, anyway?—hence, it was not thought necessary to mention such a thing when membership requirements were framed. Members could attend meetings in common and, afterwards, share the same sherry and biscuits. Thus, the unmentioned restriction was indeed implicit.

But what should Bennett do about all this? Heyward's end of the correspondence is not available. But the solution is apparent in the *Year Book*. The editors retained in the membership list the name of "Mr. Jean Toomer" of Washington, D.C. (The "Mr." might in itself be considered an adequate disguise.), and omitted entirely the notices of books by members. The rest was to be, they undoubtedly hoped, silence.

And such seems to have been the case. A survey of a good many of the contemporary reviews of *Cane* (including a notice by Braithwaite) [4] reveals not a single reference to the author's being a member of the Poetry Society of South Carolina. In fact, one reviewer staunchly maintained that "Jean Toomer" is really a pen-name for Waldo Frank! [5]

---

[4] William Stanley Braithwaite, "The Negro in Literature," *Crisis,* XXVIII (September, 1924), 210.
[5] Bruno Lasker, "Doors Opened Southward," *Survey,* LI (November 1, 1923), 190–91.

"Just Americans"

No Negro can legally marry a white woman in any Southern State. But Wisconsin does not mind, nor California. Last week at Carmel, Calif., "Provincetown of the Pacific Coast," there was an intellectual charivari. A parade of Carmel artists and authors marched to the cottage of Jean Toomer, 36, Negro philosopher (*Cane*), psychologist and lecturer, and Novelist Margery Bodine Latimer (*This Is My Body*), 33. It had just been revealed that they were married four months ago at Portage, Wis. Bridegroom Toomer, who has a small mustache and few Negroid characteristics, told the story of their romance.

One of Jean Toomer's grandfathers was Pinckney Benton Stewart Pinchback, a mulatto carpet-bagger who became Acting Governor of Louisiana but was refused a U.S. Senate seat in 1876. After attending the University of Wisconsin, Jean Toomer became an exponent of Georges Gurdjieff, the Armenian-Greek cultist who founded the Institute for the Harmonious Development of Man at Fontainebleau, France, and whose most famed disciple was the late Katherine Mansfield (TIME, March 24, 1930). Last autumn Disciple Toomer took a mixed party of eight, all white except himself, to a farmhouse outside Portage, birthplace of Novelist Latimer. She was one of the party. All slept in two rooms on cots, following the Gurdjieff method, made themselves uncomfortable to break down thought and body habits, sat around nights discussing their reactions.

"As a result of the experiment," said Jean Toomer last week, "I am satisfied that it is entirely possible to eradicate the false veneer of civilization with its unnatural inhibitions, its selfishness, petty meanness and unnatural behavior. . . . Adults can be re-educated to become as natural as little children, before civilization stamps out their true or subconscious instincts. I am satisfied that an interior life exists in all of us, a true life which will come to the surface under proper conditions."

Early in the experiment, he added, he discovered that his own reaction drew him to Novelist Latimer, likewise a onetime Wis-

Reprinted from *Time*, XIX (March 28, 1932), 19, by permission of TIME, The Weekly Newsmagazine. Copyright Time, Inc., 1932.

consin student, who first heard of her future husband when she submitted articles to a magazine he edited. They were married. So re-educated had one member of the experimental houseparty become—Newspaperwoman Sara Roberts—that she neglected to report the nuptials.

"Americans probably do not realize it," Bridegroom Toomer told his callers last week, "but there are no racial barriers any more, because there are so many Americans with strains of Negro, Indian and Oriental blood. As I see America, it is like a great stomach into which are thrown the elements which make up the life blood. From this source is coming a distinct race of people. They will achieve tremendous works of art, literature and music. They will not be white, black or yellow—just Americans."

"You do not protest against a person's religion," concluded his bride. "Why should you judge people by their color? I and hundreds of others have taken my husband for what he is—a brilliant man."

2. Introductions to Editions of *Cane*

Waldo Frank

Foreword [to the 1923 Edition of *Cane*]

Reading this book, I had the vision of a land, heretofore sunk in the mists of muteness, suddenly rising up into the eminence of song. Innumerable books have been written about the South; some good books have been written in the South. This book *is* the South. I do not mean that *Cane* covers the South or is the South's full voice. Merely this: a poet has arisen among our American youth who has known how to turn the essences and materials of his Southland into the essences and materials of literature. A poet has arisen in that land who writes, not as a Southerner, not as a rebel against Southerners, not as a Negro, not as apologist or priest or critic: who writes as a *poet*. The fashioning of beauty is ever foremost in his inspiration: not forcedly but simply, and because these ultimate aspects of his world are to him more real than all its specific problems. He has made songs and lovely stories of his land . . . not of its yesterday, but of its immediate life. And that has been enough.

How rare this is will be clear to those who have followed with concern the struggle of the South toward literary expression, and the particular trial of that portion of its folk whose skin is dark. The gifted Negro has been too often thwarted from becoming a poet because his world was forever forcing him to recollect that he was a Negro. The artist must lose such lesser identities in the great well of life. The English poet is not forever protesting and recalling that he is English. It is so natural and easy for him to be English that he can sing as a man. The French novelist is not forever noting: "This is French." It is so atmospheric for him to be French, that he can devote himself to saying: "This is human." This is an imperative condition for the creating of deep art. The whole will and mind of the creator must go below the surfaces of race. And this has been an almost impossible condition for the American Negro to achieve, forced every moment of his life into a specific and superficial plane of consciousness.

Reprinted from *Cane* by Jean Toomer (New York: Liveright Publishers, 1923), by permission of the publisher. Copyright (R) 1951 by Jean Toomer.

The first negative significance of *Cane* is that this so natural and restrictive state of mind is completely lacking. For Toomer, the Southland is not a problem to be solved; it is a field of loveliness to be sung: the Georgia Negro is not a downtrodden soul to be uplifted; he is material for gorgeous painting: the segregated self-conscious brown belt of Washington is not a topic to be discussed and exposed; it is a subject of beauty and of drama, worthy of creation in literary form.

It seems to me, therefore, that this is a first book in more ways than one. It is a harbinger of the South's literary maturity: of its emergence from the obsession put upon its minds by the unending racial crisis—an obsession from which writers have made their indirect escape through sentimentalism, exoticism, polemic, "problem" fiction, and moral melodrama. It marks the dawn of direct and unafraid creation. And, as the initial work of a man of twenty-seven, it is the harbinger of a literary force of whose incalculable future I believe no reader of this book will be in doubt.

How typical is *Cane* of the South's still virgin soil and of its pressing seeds! and the book's chaos of verse, tale, drama, its rhythmic rolling shift from lyrism to narrative, from mystery to intimate pathos! But read the book through and you will see a complex and significant form take substance from its chaos. Part One is the primitive and evanescent black world of Georgia. Part Two is the threshing and suffering brown world of Washington, lifted by opportunity and contact into the anguish of self-conscious struggle. Part Three is Georgia again . . . the invasion into this black womb of the ferment seed: the neurotic, educated, spiritually stirring Negro. As a broad form this is superb, and the very looseness and unexpected waves of the book's parts make *Cane* still more *South*, still more of an æsthetic equivalent of the land.

What a land it is! What an Aeschylean beauty to its fateful problem! Those of you who love our South will find here some of your love. Those of you who know it not will perhaps begin to understand what a warm splendor is at last at dawn.

> A feast of moon and men and barking hounds,
> An orgy for some genius of the South
> With bloodshot eyes and cane-lipped scented mouth
> Surprised in making folk-songs. . . .

So, in his still sometimes clumsy stride (for Toomer is finally a poet in prose) the author gives you an inkling of his revelation. An

individual force, wise enough to drink humbly at this great spring
of his land ... such is the first impression of Jean Toomer. But
beyond this wisdom and this power (which shows itself perhaps
most splendidly in his complete freedom from the sense of persecution), there rises a figure more significant: the artist, hard, self-
immolating, the artist who is not interested in races, whose domain
is Life. The book's final Part is no longer "promise"; it is achievement. It is no mere dawn: it is a bit of the full morning. These
materials ... the ancient black man, mute, inaccessible, and yet
so mystically close to the new tumultuous members of his race, the
simple slave Past, the shredding Negro Present, the iridescent
passionate dream of the To-morrow ... are made and measured by
a craftsman into an unforgettable music. The notes of his counterpoint are particular, the themes are of intimate connection with
us Americans. But the result is that abstract and absolute thing
called Art.

Arna Bontemps

Introduction¹ [to the 1969 Edition of *Cane*]

Looking back on the Harlem Renaissance of the 1920's, the
distinguished scholar and sociologist, Charles S. Johnson, observed
that "A brief ten years have developed more confident self-expression, more widespread efforts in the direction of art than the long,
dreary two centuries before." Recalling the sunburst of Jean
Toomer's first appearance, he added, "Here was triumphantly the

Reprinted from "Introduction" by Arna Bontemps, to *Cane* by Jean Toomer.
Perennial Classic Edition (Liveright Publishers, 1923), pp. vii-x, xii-xvi, by
permission of Harper and Row, Publishers, Inc. Introduction Copyright
© 1969 by Arna Bontemps.
¹ Several paragraphs of this essay originally appeared, in a slightly different
form, in "The Negro Renaissance: Jean Toomer and the Harlem Writers of
the 1920's," by Arna Bontemps, in *Anger, and Beyond: The Negro Writer
in the United States,* edited with an Introduction by Herbert Hill (New
York: Harper & Row, Publishers, 1966).

Negro artist, detached from propaganda, sensitive only to beauty. Where [Paul Laurence] Dunbar gave to the unnamed Negro peasant a reassuring touch of humanity, Toomer gave to the peasant a passionate charm. . . . More than artist, he was an experimentalist, and this last quality has carried him away from what was, perhaps, the most astonishingly brilliant beginning of any Negro writer of this generation."

Cane, the book that provoked this comment, was published in 1923 after portions of it had appeared earlier in *Broom*, *The Crisis*, *Double Dealer*, *Liberator*, *Little Review*, *Modern Review*, *Nomad*, *Prairie* and *S 4 N*. But *Cane* and its author, let it be said at once, presented an enigma from the start—an enigma which has, in many ways, deepened in the years since its publication. Given such a problem, perhaps one may be excused for not wishing to separate completely the man from his work.

During the summer of 1922 Toomer had sent a batch of unpublished manuscripts to the editors of the *Liberator*, Max Eastman and his assistant Claude McKay. They accepted some of the pieces enthusiastically and requested biographical material from the author. Toomer responded with the following:

Whenever the desire to know something about myself comes from a sincere source, I am always glad to meet it. For in telling folks I invariably tell my own self something. My family is from the South. My mother's father, P. B. S. Pinchback, born in Macon, Georgia, left home as a boy and worked on the Mississippi River steamers. At the beginning of the Civil War he organized and was commissioned captain of a Negro company in New Orleans. Later, in the days of Reconstruction, he utilized the Negro's vote and won offices for himself, the highest being that of lieutenant, and then acting governor of Louisiana. When his heyday was over, he left the old hunting grounds and came to Washington. Here I was born. My own father likewise came from Middle Georgia. Racially, I seem to have (who knows for sure) seven blood mixtures: French, Dutch, Welsh, Negro, German, Jewish, and Indian. Because of these, my position in America has been a curious one. I have lived equally amid the two race groups. Now white, now colored. From my own point of view I am naturally and inevitably an American. I have strived for a spiritual fusion analagous to the fact of racial intermingling. Without denying a single element in me, with no desire to subdue one to the other, I have sought to let them function as complements. I have tried to let them live in harmony. Within the last two or three years, however, my growing need for artistic expression has pulled me deeper and deeper into the Negro group.

And as my powers of receptivity increased, I found myself loving it in a way that I could never love the other. It has stimulated and fertilized whatever creative talent I may contain within me. A visit to Georgia last fall was the starting point of almost everything of worth that I have done. I heard folk-songs come from the lips of Negro peasants. I saw the rich dusk beauty that I had heard many false accents about, and of which till then, I was somewhat skeptical. And a deep part of my nature, a part that I had repressed, sprang suddenly to life and responded to them. Now, I cannot conceive of myself as aloof and separated. My point of view has not changed; it has deepened, it has widened. Personally, my life has been torturous and dispersed. The comparative wealth which my family once had, has now dwindled away to almost nothing. We, or rather, they, are in the unhappy position of the lowered middle-class. There seems to have been no shop-keepers or shysters among us. I have lived by turn in Washington, New York, Chicago, Sparta, Georgia, and several smaller towns. I have worked, it seems to me, at everything: selling papers, delivery boy, soda clerk, salesman, shipyard worker, librarian-assistant, physical director, school teacher, grocery clerk, and God knows what all. Neither the universities of Wisconsin or New York gave me what I wanted, so I quit them. Just how I finally found my stride in writing, is difficult to lay hold of. It has been pushing through for the past four years. For two years, now, I have been in solitude here in Washington. It may be begging hunger to say that I am staking my living on my work. So be it. The mould is cast, and I cannot turn back even if I would.

Neither the editors of the *Liberator* nor the lonely youth taking care of his decrepit grandparents in Washington, watching them slowly deteriorate after having led exciting and eventful lives, could have realized that this sudden outpouring was itself a strange harbinger. *Cane* was published the following year. While a few sensitive and perceptive people went quietly mad, as the saying goes, about this wholly extraordinary book, they seemed unable to enlarge its audience. Only two small printings were issued, and these vanished quickly. However, among the most affected was practically an entire generation of young Negro writers then just beginning to emerge; their reaction to Toomer's *Cane* marked an awakening that soon thereafter began to be called a Negro Renaissance. . . .

If such a first work as *Cane* was betokened by the biography he sent to his friends at the *Liberator* on August 19, 1922, it was also a harbinger of a very different sort. It foreshadowed a wild search for identity that was to drive Toomer through all the years that followed till his death in 1967 and, eventually, even to preempt his talent.

Some of Toomer's admirers, putting *Cane* beside the early work of such contemporaries as William Faulkner and Ernest Hemingway, have wondered why he appears to have stopped short and deliberately turned his back on greatness. If this was indeed what happened, a few clues as to the reasons might be cited.

As a youngster Toomer had been fascinated by the idea of self-improvement by body–building and he had enrolled in correspondence courses. His efforts had been remarkably successful, and the beautiful child of Nina Pinchback, daughter of a controversial celebrity, had grown into a personable and athletic youth. By the time of *Cane's* publication in 1923, he had turned to an intensive study of his own psychology, and in the same year encountered the ideas of Georges Ivanovitch Gurdjieff, a system or teaching by which one sought to attain through instruction and discipline new levels of experience, beginning with the difficult first step to self-consciousness and progressing to world- and possibly cosmic-consciousness. A year later he spent the summer at the Gurdjieff Institute at Fontainebleau, France, explaining to his friends, "I am. What I am and what I may become I am trying to find out."

Half a dozen years passed and he had still not resolved this problem when in 1931 he undertook a psychological experiment with a group of friends living in a cottage in Portage, Wisconsin. Not too much is known about this, and one can only assume it was in line with the Gurdjieff aims. The townsfolk, probably fearing that the "experiment" was a disguise for some sort of free love adventure, were horrified, though they pressed no accusations. A year later, Toomer married Marjory Latimer, a descendant of the early New England poet, Anne Bradstreet, and a renowned New England clergyman, John Cotton. She had been a member of the group of men and women associated with Toomer in the experiment, and her friendship with him had been an outgrowth. She was also known as one of the most promising young novelists in the United States. Marjory Latimer Toomer died the following year giving birth to their only child.

A sojourn in the Southwest, sometimes troubled, always questing, followed. During this time he appears to have made some prominent converts to the Gurdjieff system; Langston Hughes' poem "A House in Taos" was believed by some to have been inspired by Toomer's experiences there. In 1934, however, Toomer contracted an equally surprising second marriage. It was his destiny, apparently, to be closely linked with *Marjories*. With Marjorie Content, daughter of Harry Content, a member of the New York Stock Exchange, he appeared to vanish from literature among the tolerant Quakers of Bucks County, Pennsylvania. When next heard from, he was writing for the *Friends Intelligencer*, sometimes calling himself by his father's first name, lecturing piously to Friends' meetings, and occasionally making vague references to the racial blend in him.

An inquiry by a young Quaker friend of mine elicited a frank though guarded response from a General Secretary of the Philadelphia Yearly Meeting of the Religious Society of Friends. At a time when the committee that was running the George School would not permit the faculty to accept Negro applicants, someone volunteered that there was already a so-called Negro in attendance. The finger was pointed at Toomer and the child by his first wife, but Toomer parried the questions and no action was taken.

Within his own heart and mind, however, the fundamental issue was too big to be disposed of so lightly. "All of this," wrote the General Secretary, "is possibly a basis for Jean's present condition. I have recited it because of Arna Bontemps' request for biographical information for the last twenty years. He may know most of it and more, but it is during the last twenty to thirty years that I have known Jean. . . . This information was given me by Jean at my request. He did not indicate that it was confidential but it is certainly personal and should be handled in that spirit."

As this sequence occurred, Toomer made notes for an autobiography in which he proposed to cope with the problems raised by his situation. It was never developed fully, but his outlines suggest that he remembered vividly the ordeal of muscle-building in which he had engaged as a boy, his restoration after an exhausting "spell of sex," his growing disgust with "most of the life" around him in Washington, his painful vigil while watching "Pinchback's break-up," and the decline of their once well-to-do family into poverty, and eventually the grueling confrontation with himself on setting out for the University of Wisconsin. "I would again be entering a white world; and, though I personally had experienced no prejudice or exclusion either from the whites or the colored people, I had seen enough to know that America viewed life as if it were divided into white and black. Having lived with colored people for the past five years, at Wisconsin the question might come up.

What was I? I thought about it independently, and, on the basis of fact, concluded I was neither white nor black, but simply an American. I held this view and decided to live according to it. I would tell others if the occasion demanded it."

On November 7, 1923, Allen Tate, then a member of the Fugitives and one of the editors of *The Fugitive*, wrote to Jean Toomer at the suggestion of their mutual friend Hart Crane. Tate wrote him again in May 1924. Both times it was connected with a train stopover in Washington which he thought would provide an opportunity for them to meet face to face. But it never happened. Tate appears to have been reaching toward Toomer, tentatively and vaguely, on behalf of the Fugitive enclave. Had they met, perhaps some good might have resulted, both to them and to him.

Between these two attempts to meet Toomer, Tate reviewed *Cane* for the Nashville *Tennessean*, saying that parts of it "challenge some of the best modern writing," and that he judged it "highly important for literature." It was a perceptive and prophetic reading of a timeless book.

3. Contemporary Reviews

A. White Reviewers

John Armstrong

The Real Negro

"Cane" is a volume of short stories studded with poetry that is instantly identified with the "Little Review" and "Broom" schools of emotional expansion. It is a most unusual and colorful volume, too, notwithstanding its poetic lapses into naive incoherency. It is a volume depicting what one is convinced are the real negroes of the South, negroes altogether removed from the Octavus Roy Cohen and Irvin Cobb sort of inadequate caricatures. Some of the stories possess a sweep of emotional power saturated with a moist lyric beauty that positively sings. The heavy, languorous beauty of the book as a whole stuns the intelligence entirely, lulls it into torpor and compels it to recognize the authenticity of the racy negroes delineated.

Here are the high-brown and black and half-cast colored folk of the canefields, the gin hovel and the brothel realized with a sure touch of artistry. The religious fervor of the negro that affords solace of a sort in lieu of his spiritual bankruptcy is present in every page of the book. Here one becomes acquainted with the old negro who tosses "religious fits" on the street corner of some old Georgia town while the morbidly curious population gathers about and applauds his ecstasy. Here is the hysteria and emotional pandemonium akin to it prevalent in the negro camp-meeting; and the superstitions of the negro and his fear of white exploitation and persecution are painted with all of the negro's hitherto inarticulate woe accentuated.

It can perhaps be safely said that the Southern negro, at least, has found an authentic lyric voice in Jean Toomer; a voice and a heart, likewise, that is synchronized with the aspirations, the hopes and fears of the genuine darky. There is nothing of the theatrical coon-strutting high-brown, none of the conventional dice-throwing, chicken-stealing nigger of musical comedy and burlesque in the pages of "Cane." Even the recent attempt of Broadway to cap-

---

Reprinted from *New York Tribune,* October 14, 1923, p. 26, by permission of the W.C.C. Publishing Company, Inc.

italize the wealth of folk-lore and music latent in the negro spirit
is here outdone with a bravado that smacks of audacity.

These negroes drawn by Mr. Toomer seem to breathe their native air, they seem to express themselves with a vigorous, earthy
resonance of emotion that rationalizes our previous conceptions of
that race gathered from bogus sources. The negro, heretofore, has
been libeled rather than depicted accurately in American fiction,
libeled because it was supposed that he was an eternally funny sort
of fellow, always shooting craps and singing "blues" songs and
wearing gaudy neckties with big diamonds in them and stealing
chickens from any hen-coop he came across. He was never presented as a human being possessed of spirit and an identity. He
was seldom ever presented to white eyes with any other sort of
intelligence than that displayed by an idiot child with epilepsy.

Nevertheless, it has always been felt that there are negroes in
America with genuine poetic feeling, intellect and discrimination
approximating the standards of the more civilized whites. One has
always known this and wondered, likewise, why they were never
presented in our fiction. Seemingly until this book was written no
one has had the courage or perhaps the inclination to seek out
these real negroes and hold them up to view honestly.

It is patent that the author has yet a lot to learn about eluci-
dating his sometimes rather strident reactions to the negro, for at
moments his outbursts of emotion approach the inarticulately
maudlin. Yet the negro under religious emotion does evolve himself into a sort of pathological entity, and perhaps this criticism is
unjust. Nevertheless, the difficulty the author encounters is apparent, for to paint the emotional color and vivacity of the negro
requires a resource of sensibility whose ultimate dimensions often
escape rather than are captured by the pursuing word.

However, the author of "Cane" has created a distinct achievement wholly unlike anything of this sort done before. The book
is, indeed, a spiritual chronicle of the negro that was expected
long ago.

Bruno Lasker

Doors Opened Southward

[This is a joint review of Waldo Frank's *Holiday* and Toomer's *Cane*. In the passage omitted the reviewer praises *Holiday* for "penetrating to the heart" of Southern race relations and prophesies that the book will fifty years hence be seen as "a new landmark."]

Some outstanding recent contributions to the literature of race relations came up for discussion the other day. It was agreed that much of that literature is worthless—and not least that part of it which has been planned on the most extensive and "scientific" lines. The reason for this was found to lie in the curious distortion of judgment which so often takes place when people are "looking for facts," when they are trying to present these "without bias" in the light of cold abstraction rather than warm emotional interest. For example, if you were to take H. G. Wells's personal likes and dislikes out of his Outline of History, you would have left a jumble of statements concerning the development of civilization not only less appealing but also less true. An album of photographs of Rembrandt's fellow citizens would tell us less about them than his drawings and paintings—unless the photographer happened to be as great an artist.

So it is that the social student is becoming more and more dubious of the value of fact surveys made in a spirit of quasi-scientific aloofness. He finds that too often material conditions are described in tedious detail and mental states hardly touched upon at all. But in most cases it is exactly the psychology of the situation—which the ordinary technique of the surveyor usually does not suffice to ascertain—that contains the more important "facts."

All this in preface of a request for a new kind of approach by social workers to what is usually called "social fiction." Too often such literature is regarded merely as additional documentary evidence concerning conditions, less reliable than the specialist's report because the novelist lacks the investigator's training, is free to modify the record of his observations to suit his artistic aim. But it is a mistake to read the social novel as though it were inferior

---

Reprinted from *The Survey*, LI (November 1, 1923), 190–91.

sociology. Art has its own truth, far more penetrating often than
the truth of photographic description. Often it has a deeper understanding, a truer interpretation of motives and behavior. . . .

Compared with Holiday, Cane is fragmentary. In this medley of
poems, sketches and short stories, Frank—for is not "Jean
Toomer" a polite fiction?—exhibits the methods of his workshop
rather than his finished product. (By the way, we here assume
the attitude of a certain critic in the present Rembrandt contro-
versy who said, "What does it matter whether Rembrandt painted
those pictures or Bols, so long as they are genuine Rembrandts!")
But as many prefer Rembrandt's pen scratchings on bits of paper
to his paintings, so some readers will find even greater beauty and
more truth in these fragments from the emotional life of colored
folks picked up at random in the streets of a little Georgia town,
of Washington and of Chicago.

Both books give us lifelike portrayals of the American Negro,
somewhat exaggerated no doubt on the sensual side, somewhat
insufficient on the intellectual, because of the method employed.
The picture of Negro mentality obtained by the average investigator with his notebook is almost always over-rationalized. Frank-
Toomer has not interviewed him, has not asked opinions about
him, has not drawn conclusions about him from his reactions to
outside stimuli, but has made the much more searching, the much
more self-forgetting effort of seeing life with him, through him.
How rare the faculty is for doing this successfully, must be evident
to any student of the literature on race relations. Maybe our author has not succeeded completely either; maybe his models were
chosen from too limited a sympathy, seen in too limited a circle of
moods. But what there is of interpretation has the quality of life
and, thereby, of truth. Here is a sample from Holiday. The Negro,
walking to work in the morning, enters the white world:

> The path's a road. Rail fences, telegraph posts, imported Duroc
> hogs red as the clay they snout . . . a mile of farm and orchard dis-
> daining Nazareth. Lean pines cupped for the turpentine, tall blood-
> less trees rising like white folk from the cloudy earth . . . a gully dry
> and lush, spanned by an iron bridge (niggers built it and twenty
> white men have their names on the plate) . . . white Nazareth.

Anonymous

A Review of *Cane*

Sketches, short stories of a sort, poetry breathing the eternal courage of the black race, something akin to a drama, unusual in its method, these make up Mr. Toomer's volume. It is a rather curious concoction. It tries to be impressionistic, and is bedeviled by a flaming green and purple moonrise in African jungle jacket, which is even worse than the worst of the volume. It runs to stuff like this: "Fern. Face flowed into her eyes. Flowed in soft cream foam and plaintive ripples, in such a way that wherever your glance may momentarily have rested, it immediately thereafter wavered in the direction of her eyes." Or "Rhobert. Rhobert wears a house, like a monstrous diver's helmet, on his head. . . . He is way down. Rods of the house, like antennae of a dead thing, stuffed, prop up into the air. He is way down. He is sinking. His house is a dead thing that weights him down. He is sinking as a diver would sink in mud should the water be drawn off. Life is a murky, wiggling, microscopic water that compresses him. Compresses his helmet and would crush it the minute that he pulled his head out. He has to keep it in. Life is water that is being drawn off." Or "Houses are shy girls whose eyes shine reticently upon the dusk-body of the street. Upon the gleaming limbs and asphalt torso of a dreaming nigger. Shake your curled wool-blossoms, nigger. Open your liver lips to the lean, white spring."

But again he becomes articulate. "Theatre" is a vivid mob scene of innocent, unintentioned lust in a dance hall. Kabnis is the white fighting the black in the negro blood. The best thing, because the most genuine, a little verse called "Carma":

> Wind is in the cane. Come along.
> Cane leaves swaying, rusty with talk.
> Scratching choruses above the guinea's squawk.
> Wind is in the cane. Come along.

Probably this volume is a daring overflow, for it presents the black race as we seldom dare represent it, mournful, loving beauty, ignorant, and full of passion untutored and entirely unconnected with the brain.

Reprinted from *Boston Transcript,* December 15, 1923, p. 8, by permission of Mr. F. Gregg Bemis.

Robert Littell

A Review of *Cane*

"Reading this book," says Mr. Waldo Frank in his introduction, "I had the vision of a land, heretofore sunk in the mists of muteness, suddenly rising up into the eminence of song. . . . This book *is* the South." Not the South of the chivalrous gentleman, the fair lady, the friendly, decaying mansion, of mammies, cotton and pickaninnies. Nor yet the South of lynchings and hatreds, of the bitter, rebellious young Negro, and of his emigration to the North. Cane does not remotely resemble any of the familiar, superficial views of the South on which we have been brought up. On the contrary, Mr. Toomer's view is unfamiliar and bafflingly subterranean, the vision of a poet far more than the account of things seen by a novelist—lyric, symbolic, oblique, seldom actual.

In many respects, Mr. Toomer recalls Waldo Frank. They seem curiously to coincide at their weakest points. Such sentences as these might have been written by either of them: "Dark swaying forms of Negroes are street-songs that woo virginal houses . . . Dan Moore walks southward on Thirteenth Street . . . girl eyes within him widen upward to promised faces . . . Negroes open gates and go indoors, perfectly." Such phrases mean either almost nothing, or a great deal too much. In the case of Mr. Frank they seem to contain, bottled up within them, the very essence of what he wants to say; in the case of Mr. Toomer, they are occasional, accidental, and could be brushed off without damage to the whole. While Mr. Toomer often tries for puzzling and profound effects, he accomplishes fairly well what he sets out to do, and Cane is not seething, like nearly all Mr. Frank's books, with great inexpressible things bursting to be said, and only occasionally arriving, like little bubbles to the surface of a sea of molten tar.

Cane is sharply divided into two parts. The first is a series of sketches, almost poetic in form and feeling, revolving about a character which emerges with very different degrees of clarity. The second half is a longish short story, Kabnis, quite distinct from the sketches, and peculiarly interesting. In this Mr. Toomer shows a genuine gift for character portrayal and dialogue. In the sketches,

Reprinted from *The New Republic*, XXXVII (December 26, 1923), 126, by permission of Anita Littell.

the poet is uppermost. Many of them begin with three or four lines of verse, and end with the same lines, slightly changed. The construction here is musical, too often a little artificially so. The body of the sketch tends to poetry, and to a pattern which begins to lose its effectiveness as soon as one guesses how it is coming out. The following, which is about a third of one of the sketches, is a fair sample of Mr. Toomer writing at his best:

> Her soul is like a little thrust-tailed dog that follows her, whimpering. She is large enough, I know, to find a warm spot for it. But each night when she comes home and closes the big outside storm door, the little dog is left in the vestibule, filled with chills till morning. Some one . . . eoho Jesus . . . soft as a cotton ball brushed against the milk-pod cheek of Christ, will steal in and cover it that it need not shiver, and carry it to her where she sleeps upon clean hay cut in her dreams.

It isn't necessary, to know exactly what this means in order to find pleasure in reading it. Which is one way of defining poetry. And once we begin to regard Mr. Toomer's shorter sketches as poetry, many objections to the obscurer symbolism and obliqueness of them disappear. There remains, however, a strong objection to their staccato beat. The sentences fall like small shot from a high tower. They pass from poetry into prose, and from there into Western Union.

Kabnis, the longest piece in the book, is far the most direct and most living, perhaps because it seems to have grown so much more than been consciously made. There is no pattern in it, and very little effort at poetry. And Mr. Toomer makes his Negroes talk like very real people, almost, in spots, as if he had taken down their words as they came. A strange contrast to the lyric expressionism of the shorter pieces. A real peek into the mind of the South, which, like nearly all such genuinely intimate glimpses, leaves one puzzled, and—fortunately—unable to generalize.

Cane is an interesting, occasionally beautiful and often queer book of exploration into old country and new ways of writing.

Anonymous

Literary Vaudeville
[A Review of *Cane*]

Fond of vaudeville? Vaudeville is what Jean Toomer's "Cane" (Boni & Liveright) is called by its publishers. "Its acts are sketches, short stories, one long drama, and a few poems." The entertainment before the intermission is concerned with the folk-life of the Southern Negro; that after the intermission, with the "brown life" of Washington. The drama is an "added attraction." Waldo Frank writes a foreword for the volume. He says:—

"This book is the South. I do not mean that 'Cane' covers the South or is the South's full voice. Merely this: A poet has arisen among our American youth who has known how to turn essences and materials of his Southland into the essences and materials of literature. He has made songs and lovely stories of his land."

The reader not possessed of the key to ejaculatory expressionism and impressionism will find some of this vaudeville hard to follow. He may think that in some of it there is more of the showman than of the actor and his part.

Reprinted from *Springfield Republican,* December 23, 1923, p. 9a, by permission of Mr. Sidney Cook and the Springfield Newspapers.

B. Black Reviewers

Montgomery Gregory

A Review of *Cane*

The recent publication of "Cane" marks a distinct departure in southern literature and at the same time introduces a writer of extraordinary power in the person of Jean Toomer. Few books of recent years have greater significance for American letters than this "first" work of a young Negro, the nephew of an acting reconstruction governor of Louisiana. Fate has played another of its freakish pranks in decreeing that southern life should be given its most notable artistic expression by the pen of a native son of Negro descent.

It is a notorious fact that the United States south of the Mason and Dixon line has been, in the words of Mr. Mencken, a "Cultural Sahara." First torn and rent by the ravages of one of the most destructive civil strifes in all history, the states of the former confederacy have either used up their creative powers in mending the wreckage or have consumed them in the blighting fires of race hatred. The white South, with few exceptions, has sacrificed art for propaganda. Great art, like great deeds, cannot flourish in a land of bigotry and oppression. The great exception to this general indictment of the white South, Joel Chandler Harris, drew his material and his inspiration for his "Uncle Remus" stories from the unembittered and kindly lips of a former slave.

The Negro, altho immersed in the miasma of southern prejudice, because of his natural gentleness of soul and kindness of heart, suffers less from its pestilential influence than his white brother. Behold Paul Laurence Dunbar singing the plaintive songs of his people in immortal verse before the smoke of battle had cleared from the fields of Gettysburg and the Wilderness. Yet the Negro has been too conscious of his wrongs, too sensitive to oppression to be able to express the beauty of his racial life or to glorify his native soil. He has likewise resented the use of his folk-life for artistic purposes. It has been conceded that the varied life of the Negro in America, especially his folk-life, offers almost unparalleled

Reprinted from "Our Book Shelf," *Opportunity,* I (December, 1923), 374–75.

opportunities for the brush of the artist and the pen of the poet.
Max Rheinhardt [sic], the world's premier dramatic director, during his recent visit to this country, stated that the chief contribution
of America to the drama of tomorrow would be its development of
Negro folk-drama. But what has been the attitude of the Negro
himself? Unqualified opposition to the utilization of his mass life
in fiction, in music, or in drama.

What has this attitude meant? It has robbed the race of its
birthright for a mess of pottage. It has damned the possibilities of
true artistic expression at its very source. It has enabled the white
artist to exploit the Negro race for personal recognition or commercial gain. Instead of a faithful and sympathetic portrayal of our
race-life by our own artists, we have been the victims of this alien
exploitation, with the result that caricatures of the race have been
accepted as bona fide portraits.

Art is *self-expression*. The artist can only truly express his own
soul or the race-soul. Not until Rene Maran, a Negro, had pictured
the native life of Africa in "Batouala," did the dark continent find
a true exponent of its wrongs and of its resentment against a cruel
bondage. The white missionary or itinerant visitor had always
described the natives in the light of his own preconceived prej-
udices.

America has waited for its own counterpart of Maran—for that
native son who would avoid the pitfalls of propaganda and moraliz-
ing on the one hand and the snares of a false and hollow race pride
on the other hand. One whose soul mirrored the soul of his people,
yet whose vision was universal.

Jean Toomer, the author of "Cane," is in a remarkable manner
the answer to this call. Sprung from the tangy soil of the South, he
combines the inheritance of the old Negro and the spirit of the new
Negro. His grandfather, P. B. S. Pinchback, was acting governor of
Louisiana and later settled in Washington where his grandson, Jean
Toomer, was born in 1894. Thus his childhood was spent in a home
where dramatic incidents of slavery, of the Civil War and of Reconstruction, were household traditions. The "Song of the Son,"
one of the several exquisite lyrics that appear in "Cane," shows
the deep affection which young Toomer has for the old South:

> "An everlasting song, a singing tree,
> Caroling softly souls of slavery,
> What they were, and what they are to me,
> Caroling softly souls of slavery."

A youth rich in wide human experience and marked by a natural love for solitude followed. Later came an opportunity to teach at a small school in Georgia, where he secured the contacts with life in the South which were to give him his final inspirations for the book which is the subject of this criticism. "I felt strange, as I always do in Georgia, particularly at dusk. I felt that things unseen to men were tangibly immediate. It would not have surprised me had I had a vision. . . . When one is on the soil of one's ancestors, most anything can come to one."

"Cane" is not to be classified in terms of the ordinary literary types, for the genius of creation is evident in its form. Verse, fiction, and drama are fused into a spiritual unity, an "aesthetic equivalent" of the Southland. It is not a book to be intellectually understood; it must be emotionally, aesthetically felt. One must approach it with all of his five senses keenly alive if appreciation and enjoyment are to result. No previous writer has been able in any such degree to catch the sensuous beauty of the land or of its people or to fathom the deeper spiritual stirrings of the mass-life of the Negro. "Cane" is not OF the South, it is not OF the Negro; it IS the South, it IS the Negro—as Jean Toomer has experienced them. It may be added that the pictures do not pretend to be the only possible ones in such a vast panorama of life. "The Emperor Jones" was a study of one Negro as Eugene O'Neill saw him. That only. So with "Cane." It cannot be justly criticized because it does not harmonize with your personal conceptions, Mr. Reader!

"Cane" has three main divisions. The first division is laid in the land of cane, cotton and sawdust piles—Georgia. The second part deals with the more sophisticated life of the Negro "world within a world" in Washington. The third section is an intense drama of all the complicated elements of southern life, with its setting also in Georgia.

The writer will be pardoned for expressing his decided preference for the sketches, stories, and poems which compromise part one. Here the matchless beauty of the folk-life of the southern Negro is presented with intriguing charm. It is realism—not of the reportorial type found in "Main Street" writing—but the higher realism of the emotions. Here we have that mysterious, subtle and incomprehensible appeal of the South made all the more interesting because of the discordant and chaotic human elements submerged there. Of course, one is conscious of the protest of those who confuse superficial and transitory political and economic conditions with the underlying eternal elements. Those with an eye

for beauty, an ear for music, and a heart for emotion, while ab-
horring the temporary victimizing of the South by unscrupulous
demagogues, must still appreciate the fundamental Beauty which
is revealed in "Cane."

The power of portraiture is unmistakable. No effort is made to
create ideal characters or to make them conform to any particular
standard. Here we have the method of Maran and all great artists.
The characters appear in all of their lovable human qualities. We
love them and yet pity them for human weaknesses for which not
they but their ignorance and environment are largely responsible.
It is not a question of morality but of life.

Toomer appreciates as an artist the surpassing beauty, both
physical and spiritual, of the Negro woman and he has unusual
facility of language in describing it. There is "Karintha at twenty,
carrying beauty, perfect as the dusk as the sun goes down." A way-
ward child of nature whose tragedy was that "the soul of her was a
growing thing ripened too soon." Of "Carma" it is said, "She does
not sing; her body is a song." I prefer "Fern" to all the other portraits because the author has succeeded in conveying exquisite
physical charm coupled with an almost divine quality of inarticulate spirituality. Sufficient tribute has never been paid to the beauty
of the Negro woman's eyes. Visitors from foreign lands have frequently pointed out this unique glory of our women. Is it any
wonder? For do not their eyes express from mysterious depths the
majesty of lost empires, the pathos of a woman's lot in slavery, and
the spirit of a resurgent race? Fern's eyes. "Face flowed into eyes.
Flowed in soft cream foam and plaintive ripples, in such a way that
wherever your glance may momentarily have rested, it immediately
thereafter wavered in the direction of her eyes. . . . If you have ever
heard a Jewish cantor sing, if he has touched you and made your
own sorrow seem trivial when compared with his, you know my
feeling when I followed the curves of her profile, the mobile rivers,
to their common delta." But her eyes were not of ordinary beauty.
"They were strange eyes. In this, that they sought nothing—that
is nothing that was obvious or tangible or that one could see. . . .
Her eyes, unusually weird and open, held me. Held God. He flowed
in as I have seen the countryside."

Mention must also be made of "Blood Burning Moon," a short
story which closes this first section. Its splendid technique and
striking theme are attested by the fact that O'Brien has included
it in his collection of the best short stories of 1923.

A series of impressionistic views of Negro life in Washington,
D.C., follows in the middle section of "Cane." Again one must be

cautioned that the beauty of the work must be captured thru the senses. Seventh Street is a "crude boned, soft-skinned wedge of nigger life breathing its loafer air, jazz songs and love, thrusting unconscious rhythms, black reddish blood into the white and white-washed wood of Washington." Thickly scattered thru these pages are unforgettable "purple patches" which reveal the animate and inanimate life of You Street thru the sensitive emotional reactions of a poet. It must also be said that the style is more labored and sometimes puzzling. One feels at times as if the writer's emotions had out-run his expression. Is it that Mr. Toomer's highest inspiration is to be found in the folk-life of his beloved Southland and that his unmistakable distaste for the cramped and strictly conventionalized life of the city Negro restricts his power of clear and forceful language? There is not the same easy rhythmic cadence of expression here as in the first division. There are also a few apparent irrelevancies (for the reader) in the text which add nothing to the total effect and detract from the artistic value of the whole. "Box Seat" which reaches high points of excellence in the portraiture of "Muriel," "Dan," and "Mrs. Pribby," and in its dramatic narrative style, limps at times with obscure writing. The thoughts attributed to "Dan," on page 124, are a case in point and strain the demand of art to the breaking point. The remaining narratives in this division are of great merit but on the whole are not of the same excellence as his chapters of Georgia life.

The drama of "Ralph Kabnis" closes the book and marks a return to Georgia. This is no ordinary drama. It can only be likened to the grimly powerful work of the Russian dramatists. Only Eugene O'Neill in America has written anything to measure up to its colossal conception. One competent critic has stated that only the Moscow Art Theatre could do justice to such a drama. It is to be hoped that a Negro Theatre will immediately arise capable of producing "Kabnis" and other plays sure to follow from Toomer.

"Kabnis" is the fitting climax to a remarkable book. Here are placed upon the stage the outstanding factors in the inner circle of Negro life. The traditional Negro is there—the Negro of the past—mute, blind, motionless, yet a figure of sphinx-like mystery and fascination. There is a type of young Negro, attractive, frivolous, and thoughtless. Then there is Kabnis himself, the talented, highly emotional, educated Negro who goes south to elevate his people but who lacks the strength of mind and character to withstand the pressure of the white South or the temptations within his own group. Finally, there is Lewis. "He is what a stronger Kabnis might have been. . . . His mouth and eyes suggest purpose

guided by an adequate intelligence." Yet he does not understand
these black people of the South and they do not understand him.
In the end he flees from the situation without in any way helping
his people who needed his help.

Evidently the author's implication is that there must be a welding into one personality of Kabnis and Lewis: the great emotionalism of the race guided and directed by a great purpose and a super-
intelligence.

"Cane" leaves this final message with me. In the South we have
a "powerful underground" race with a marvelous emotional power
which like Niagara before it was harnessed is wasting itself. Release it into proper channels, direct its course intelligently, and
you have possibilities for future achievements that challenge the
imagination. The hope of the race is in the great blind forces of the
masses properly utilized by capable leaders.

"Dan goes to the wall and places his ear against it. That rumble
comes from the earth's core. It is the mutter of powerful and underground races. . . . The next world savior is coming up that way."

W. E. B. DuBois

The Younger
Literary Movement

There have been times when we writers of the older set have
been afraid that the procession of those who seek to express the
life of the American Negro was thinning and that none were coming forward to fill the footsteps of the fathers. Dunbar is dead;
Chesnutt is silent; and Kelly Miller is mooning after false gods
while Brawley and Woodson are writing history rather than literature. But even as we ask "Where are the young Negro artists to
mold and weld this mighty material about us?"—even as we ask,
they come.

Reprinted from *The Crisis,* XXVII (February, 1924), 161–62, by permission
of the editor.

There are two books before me, which, if I mistake not, will mark an epoch: a novel by Jessie Fauset and a book of stories and poems by Jean Toomer. There are besides these, five poets writing: Langston Hughes, Countée Cullen, Georgia Johnson, Gwendolyn Bennett and Claude McKay. Finally, Negro men are appearing as essayists and reviewers, like Walter White and Eric Walrond. (And even as I write comes the news that a novel by Mr. White has just found a publisher.) Here then is promise sufficient to attract us. . . .

The world of black folk will some day arise and point to Jean Toomer as a writer who first dared to emancipate the colored world from the conventions of sex. It is quite impossible for most Americans to realize how straight-laced and conventional thought is within the Negro World, despite the very unconventional acts of the group. Yet this contradiction is true. And Jean Toomer is the first of our writers to hurl his pen across the very face of our sex conventionality. In "Cane" one has only to take his women characters *seriatim* to realize this: Here is Karintha, an innocent prostitute; Becky, a fallen white woman; Carma, a tender Amazon of unbridled desire; Fern, an unconscious wanton; Esther, a woman who looks age and bastardy in the face and flees in despair; Louise, with a white and a black lover; Avey, unfeeling and unmoral; and Doris, the cheap chorus girl. These are his women, painted with a frankness that is going to make his black readers shrink and criticize; and yet they are done with a certain splendid, careless truth.

Toomer does not impress me as one who knows his Georgia but he does know human beings; and, from the background which he has seen slightly and heard of all his life through the lips of others, he paints things that are true, not with Dutch exactness, but rather with an impressionist's sweep of color. He is an artist with words but a conscious artist who offends often by his apparently undue striving for effect. On the other hand his powerful book is filled with felicitous phrases—Karintha, "carrying beauty perfect as the dusk when the sun goes down,"—

> *"Hair—*
> *Silver-grey*
> *Like streams of stars"*

Or again, "face flowed into her eyes—flower in soft creamy foam and plaintive ripples." His emotion is for the most part entirely objective. One does not feel that he feels much and yet the fervor of his descriptions shows that he has felt or knows what feeling is. His art carries much that is difficult or even impossible to understand. The artist, of course, has a right deliberately to make his art a puzzle to the interpreter (the whole world is a puzzle) but on the other hand I am myself unduly irritated by this sort of thing. I cannot, for the life of me, for instance see why Toomer could not have made the tragedy of Carma something that I could understand instead of vaguely guess at; "Box Seat" muddles me to the last degree and I am not sure that I know what "Kabnis" is about. All of these essays and stories, even when I do not understand them, have their strange flashes of power, their numerous messages and numberless reasons for being. But still for me they are partially spoiled. Toomer strikes me as a man who has written a powerful book but who is still watching for the fullness of his strength and for that calm certainty of his art which will undoubtedly come with years.

Robert T. Kerlin

Singers of New Songs

[The following is from a joint review of Toomer's *Cane*, Langston Hughes's *The Weary Blues*, and Countée Cullen's *Color*.]

"Like purple tallow flames, songs jet up. They spread a ruddy haze over the heavens. The haze swings low. Now the whole countryside is a soft chorus." So Jean Toomer, in *Cane*, describes the effect of a song spark that traveled swiftly from cabin to cabin in a Georgia night. Not all white folks, perhaps not many, will understand it. There is more primitive poetry, and more poetic mysticism, in *Cane*, than in any other book yet produced on this continent. Further on in the story comes this:

"Slave boy whom some Christian mistress taught to read the Bible. Black man who saw Jesus in the rice fields, and began

Reprinted from *Opportunity*, IV (May, 1926), 162.

preaching to his people. Moses—and Christ—words used for songs. Dead blind father of a muted folk who feel their way upward to a life that crushes or absorbs them."

Twice have I had the kinship of the African and the Indian (or Hindu) mind impressed distinctly upon me: once and again in reading Charles H. Conner's *The Enchanted Valley* (alas! so little known!) and a second time and again in reading *Cane*. It chanced that I came to this latter book direct from Mukerju's *Caste and Outcast*. Who does not know that the Negroes have an understanding of *our* Scriptures—which of course are ours only by imperfect adoption—which leaves us wondering, and ought to leave us humiliated? But I am now speaking about poetry, not religion, though the two are not far asunder. Again I quote from *Cane:*

> "Ralph Kabnis, propped in his bed, tries to read. Ceiling, patterned by the fringed globe of the lamp. The walls, unpainted, are seasoned a rosin yellow. And cracks between the boards are black. These cracks are the lips the night winds use for whispering. Night winds in Georgia are vagrant poets, whispering. Kabnis, against his will, lets his book slip down, and listens to them."

When "an atom of dust in agony on a Georgia hillside" hears in the winds through the cracks of his cabin the whisperings of vagrant poets what may not be expected of that same "atom" when the agony, intensified, understood, has at command the language of Shakespeare, Shelley, Sandburg?

Cane is written partly in verse form, partly in prose: all of it has the spirit of poetry. It is, in respect to content and form, an audacious book, stamped all over with genius.

The story of Dunbar's printing and peddling his first book is well known. Something like that has been the story of all Negro books of verse hitherto. I have a shelf of such books—the cost of printing borne by the author, the burden of selling borne by the author. Is it not a notable event in the history of the American Negro, and of America, that in the first months of the year 1926 two young Negro poets had their books put forth, on their merits and trade value, just as white poets' books, by two publishing firms of first repute for orthodox business? Negro poets are in the market, no longer lost wanderers on Parnassus. . . .

4. Critical Essays

A. Black Critics

Eugene Holmes

Jean Toomer —
Apostle of Beauty

In writing about Toomer, one is discussing a man who has been poetically quiet for the past eight years. His importance lies in this fact, gainsaid only by J. W. Johnson, since he neglects to include him in his "Second Book of American Negro Verse"—that whether or not he has written anything recently, he remains one of the more important Negro poets. There are no major Negro poets in America. And Toomer's position is justifiable in that he has exerted a very strong influence in American literature of today.

To those who offer objections to the inclusion of Toomer in a study of modern Negro poets, I reply that because of his influence and because of the unknowableness of the future of Negro poetry no study would be complete without Toomer. We can know nothing about the future of Negro poetry simply because we can form no idea about the importance of those who are writing today. We are too close to their work and since most of the younger poets have little or no repute, all we can do is judge any work tentatively. For these reasons, it can be seen that the work of Toomer must be examined for what is in it, whether he is poetically dead or not. And the mere fact that his influence has given to many poets intelligent guidance and poetic appreciation should suffice that his work be included. Lest I appear to be Toomer's apologist, let it be said that there is ample enough poetry as poetry in his one book for him to be included in any select niche of poetical art.

Not many people in America and Europe knew the name of Jean Toomer ten years ago. The few who did know him and his verse were acquainted only if they read the *Double Dealer of New Orleans, The Little Review, Broom, The Liberator, S. N. 4, Prairie, Nomad* and "little" magazines. It was in 1923, with the publication of "Cane" that he became known to a sizeable majority of readers

Reprinted from *Opportunity,* X (August, 1932), 252–54, 260.

in this country. In "Cane" raving critics and poetasters recognized a naturalism of such a distinctive kind that the applause was deafening.

This novel element in his poetry was distinctive because first of all, here was a Negro who composed not as a Negro, but as an artist, and secondly because there was not in his poetry any obsession of race. At first, the critics could not understand that a Negro could write poetry that did not reek with rebellion and propaganda. Toomer wrote as a poet, never as an apologist. Reading the turbulent and rebellious poetry of the McKay of that time, this poetry of Toomer's came upon the poetic horizon as a breath of sweet, cool air.

Toomer possessed what Max Eastman termed "the poetic temper." His poetry mirrored a full life of experience. It contained in the fullest sense what Prof. Whipple called "social experience," the complete cognizance of other people and of all their characteristics and inner souls. In his poetry he had probed deep down into the life-experience of his characters. He saw them as they were in all their real significance and he entered into these experiences with them, translating them into the moving poetical rhythms of "Cane."

Some critic, I forget who, years ago wrote that with Toomer, "the fashioning of beauty is ever foremost in his inspiration." And that is essentially true in almost every poem he has written. Beauty is always his medium, always his goal and always for him the *summum bonum* of existence. He finds in life challenge and beauty, only beauty is uppermost. It is this preoccupation with beauty that has stamped him as an important poet. It has also given the necessary influence and impetus to those younger Negro poets who did not know about what to write.

Toomer's influence, I repeat, has been great and inspirational and has found its way down the line into the work of many of these younger Negro poets. They have been impelled to see, through Toomer's eyes, the objectives in the fashioning of beauty. They have perforce seen that in order to be a poet, it is not at all necessary to try and solve the race problem. They have been led to believe also that the interests of the true poet-artist as exemplified in Toomer must be writ large in the experiences of life, as they are separated from the materialities of existence.

Those who have followed him have seen that his poetry is always concerned with the very depths of human experience:

A feast of moon and men and barking hounds
An orgy for some genius of the South
With blood-hot eyes and cane-lipped scented mouth,
Surprised in making folk-songs from soul sounds.

In its ascendancy to universality this poetry in its tragic flight soars to greatness. He transcends the temporal and scarce worthwhile things and sings of Man:

An everlasting song, a singing tree,
Caroling softly souls of slavery.

The experiences incorporated in his poems are vividly real and are calculated to arouse the most lethargic of emotions. They stir and surge through you, effecting the katharsis that only poetry of this kind can compel. That this wealth of experience is enriched by his imagination, almost any line of his poetry will show:

"Their voices rise . . . the pine trees are guitars,"

Jean Toomer was born in Washington, D.C., in 1896. His parents were proud, cultured Negroes of old Creole stock. They had come from Louisiana to Washington in order to educate their children. In Louisiana they had been people of some consequence, in social position and wealth. But there were no opportunities for even a public school education in Louisiana. Mrs. Toomer's father was Lieutenant Governor Pinchback of Louisiana and played a great part in the Reconstruction Days of that state. Toomer received his public school education in the Washington public schools. After graduation from high school, he stayed in Washington for a while and then went West to study law. After two years at a law school, he gave it up and came to New York City. Here, he began to dabble in free-lance writing and contributing verse to "little magazines." His writings brought him into contact with such famous artists and critics as Alfred Stieglitz, Paul Rosenfeld, Waldo Frank, Gorham Munson and Max Eastman. He became a member of this select circle and took a great part in the wholesome critical attitude of the times.

In 1921, he decided, for some reason still unknown to him, to teach in Georgia. He went down there expectant, eyes and ears open, waiting to drink in whatever experiences teaching in Georgia would hold for him. In "Cane," and in his poetry he tells us just what those experiences were. Georgia, the Southland, the home of his fathers awakened in him something he had not known existed. He found down there a hereditary link with forgotten and unknown ancestors. Slavery once a shame and a stigma became for him a spiritual process of growth and transfiguration and the tortuous underground groping of one generation, the maturing and high blossoming of the next. He found in the life of those Georgians and their forebears a sense of mystical recognition. Of this dark fruit of experiences he had this to say:

> *One plum was saved for me, one seed becomes*
> *An everlasting song, a singing tree*
> *Caroling softly souls of slavery.*

He found out that there must have existed a preordained motive in his going to Georgia. He had been able to identify himself with the "souls of slavery" that had gone before him. He saw in those simple, lovely folk a garden beautiful and lovely to behold. The supreme beauty which he found there was the vast blackness into which his heart ventured—like a man who plunges into deep water. This love of simple things, as well as of humble souls, is indeed a dominant note in his song:

> *O land and soil, red soil and sweet-gum tree*
> *So scant of grass, so profligate of pines.*
> *Now just before an epoch's sun declines,*
> *Thy son, in time I have returned to thee,*
> *Thy son, I have, in time, returned to thee.*

As Gorham Munson wrote,* "It seems here that at last a wandering child had returned to his home, to the home of his fathers . . . so that he can immerse himself in the deep folk riches of the Georgia soil and so look for his soul in the earth."

His experiences in Georgia had prompted him to publish in 1923, "Cane," a book which most critics were anxious to style poetic prose. Back in New York, in the circle composed of Frank, Munson, Stieglitz, and Rosenfeld, he admits that he saw life much differently after his Georgia sojourn. He began to express dissatisfaction for American life. It seemed to be so chaotic and purposeless. Knowing inwardly that an artist's first obligation to himself is "personal

---

* "Destinations," 1928, in which a chapter is devoted to Toomer.

unification," he decided to cure himself. He began looking around him to find some means whereby he might seek a different self-expression. He began to psychoanalyze himself. Then he underwent the rigorous training prescribed by F. Matthias Alexander for "conscious control of the body." Then a summer at the Gurdjieff Institute at Fontainebleau. Here, he wrote that he had found just what he had been searching for; "I am. What I am and what I may become I am trying to find out." If that explains his poetical reticence and his Gurdjieff activities, there is nothing to say.

When Orage, Gurdjieff's representative, came to America, he took Toomer with him to Chicago where they set up an American institute. He wrote a remarkable short story, "Easter" that appeared in the 1925 Little Review. His "Values and Fictions: A Psychological Record," still unpublished, is due to appear shortly. Only a few months ago, under Gurdjieff's auspices, (privately printed) there appeared "Essentials," a book of epigrams and distiches. He says that he has not stopped writing poetry and that he will publish a volume of verse in the next few years. It will be interesting to notice what many years will have done to his poetic outlook.

Toomer had thought of becoming a composer before he turned to poetry and the novel. It is very easy to see this affinity with music. His is essentially the poet-musician's soul. Rather, he is the creative artist whose work is based on the truth of music and poetry. There is so much of musical unity in his work that the sheer artistry in it stands out vividly. Anyone who can combine vowels and liquids to form a cadence like "she was as innocently lovely as a November cotton-flower" has a subtle command of word-music. His verse is always cadenced to accord with the unusually sensitive ear.

His word-painting is based on a strict fidelity to nature, his art is founded on truth, hence its vitality. His descriptions are made on direct notations, and as he composes with the precision and vividness of an artist working with his ear close to the subject, the freshness of the first impression clings to the poem. The exactness of his notations may be seen in an epithet of color as in "Face":

> *Hair—*
> *silver gray*
> *like streams of stars,*
> *Brows—*
> *recurved canoes*

> *quivered by the ripples blown by pain,*
> *Her eyes—*
> *mist of tears*
> *condensing on the flesh below:*
>   *And her channeled muscles*
> *are cluster grapes of sorrow*
> *purple in the evening sun*
> *nearly ripe for worms.*

You cannot help seeing the face. It is evoked with a faithful precision with only a few particulars, selected with keen and original insight and painted with broad deliberate touch. I doubt if there has been such a skilful delineation done so well recently.

Toomer accepts life, yet there is in his heart a yearning for completeness and unity. There is in him a good deal of the mystic—not of the type who wants to commune with God and Nature more intimately on a mountain top—but the type who has in himself the deep aspiration for the "peace that passeth understanding."

Every poet carries his message. Toomer's is beauty and the mystery of life. He recognizes in life just so much 'sweetness and light,' color and song, pathos and tragedy, and he accepts all this because it is beautiful and mysterious. He has been wounded in life and so too have his simple, beloved people he writes about. He cares not so much for himself. For those simple, singing people, he has the deep sense of pity. He is keenly alive to their sorrows, he feels acutely the anguish and misery of man's existence, the dumb pain of nature; suffering creatures are by him passionately loved:

> *O singers, resinous and soft your songs,*
> *Above the sacred whisper of the pines,*
> *Gives virgin lips to cornfield concubines,*
> *Bring dreams of Christ to dusky cane-lipped throngs.*

His feeling of pity extends to animals and things, to the field rat who:

> *. . . startled, squealing bleeds,*
> *His belly close to ground. I see the blade*
> *Blood-stained, continue cutting weeds and shades.*

He is deeply moved by the sight of dying cotton. There is intense pathos and understanding here:

And cotton, scarce as any southern snow,
Was vanishing, the branch so pinched and slow,
Failed in its junction as the autumn rake:

He is usually placed, owing to the exactness of his notations from nature and life, among the "realists" and "naturalists." Yet "realism" or "naturalism" should have no proper meaning in art and poetry. A poet or painter or a musician always is a visionary soul, that is, they descry the "true reality" beyond appearances. Toomer can, if he wants, deny membership in this clique, for instead, he exalts the magic of reality, not of dreams. He woke up to spiritual realities, and to the ethical side of our existence. The mystic feeling added to the poetical intensity of his lives, spreading a new glow over familiar objects and surroundings. In his descriptions even the commonplace and the obvious are clothed with a new light.

I believe that Toomer's poetry will live because it is of the stuff of pure poetry. It is the great depth of emotion implicit in his poems, and the sincerity and simplicity of style that have given him a notable place among contemporary poets. We must agree with Paul Rosenfeld * when he wrote of Toomer that he "comes to unlimber a soul and give of its dance and music."

---

* Paul Rosenfeld, "Twenty-Four Men" (a chapter on Toomer).

Saunders Redding

The New Negro

... In 1923 came Jean Toomer's *Cane,* a revolutionary book that gave definiteness to the new movement and exposed a wealth of new material. A youth of twenty-eight fresh from the South when *Cane* was published, he held nothing so important to the artistic treatment of Negroes as racial kinship with them. Unashamed and

---

Reprinted from *To Make A Poet Black* (Chapel Hill: The University of North Carolina Press, 1939), pp. 104–06, by permission of the publisher. Copyright © 1939 by the University of North Carolina Press.

unrestrained, Jean Toomer loved the race and the soil that sustained it. His moods are hot, colorful, primitive, but more akin to the naïve hysteria of the spirituals than to the sophisticated savagery of jazz and the blues. *Cane* was a lesson in emotional release and freedom. Through all its prose and poetry gushes a subjective tide of love. "He comes like a son returned in bare time to take a living full farewell of a dying parent; and all of him loves and wants to commemorate that perishing naïvete." Hear how he revels in the joy and pain, the beauty and tragedy of his people:

> Pour, O pour that parting soul in song,
> O pour it in the sawdust glow of night,
> Into the velvet pine-smoke air tonight,
> And let the valley carry it along.
> And let the valley carry it along.

> O land and soil, red soil and sweet-gum tree,
> So scant of grass, so profligate of pines,
> Now just before an epoch's sun declines,
> Thy son, in time, I have returned to thee,
> Thy son, I have in time returned to thee.

> In time, for though the sun is setting on
> A song-lit race of slaves, it has not set;
> Though late, O soil, it is not too late yet
> To catch thy plaintive soul, leaving, soon gone,
> Leaving, to catch thy plaintive soul soon gone.

> O Negro slaves, dark purple ripened plums,
> Squeezed, and bursting in the pine-wood air,
> Passing, before they stripped the old tree bare
> One plum was saved for me, one seed becomes

> An everlasting song, a singing tree,
> Caroling softly souls of slavery,
> What they were, and what they are to me,
> Caroling softly souls of slavery.

Great splotches of color and sensuousness make gaudy palettes of his pages:

> A feast of moon and men and barking hounds,
>   An orgy for some genius of the South
>   With blood-hot eyes and cane-lipped scented mouth,
> Surprised in making folk-songs from soul sounds.

Cane was experimental, a potpourri of poetry and prose, in which the latter element is significant because of the influence it had on the course of Negro fiction. Mr. Toomer is indebted to Sherwood Anderson and Waldo Frank for much in his prose style, but his material is decidedly his own. Sometimes he falls short of his best abilities for lack of government, as in the story "Kabnis," which says and does much but obscures much more. Sometimes he succeeds splendidly, as in the sketches "Carma" and "Fern," in which feeling and language are restrained and genuine. But often he wallows in feeling and grows inarticulate with a rush of words.

Though *Cane* was in the nature of an experiment (the conclusion to which we are fearful of never knowing, for since 1923 Toomer has published practically nothing) it established the precedent of self-revelation that has characterized the writings of Negroes on all levels ever since. At first completely absorbed in fulfilling his opportunity for release, the new Negro had no time for new forms. In his anxiety and relief he did not reflect that he was pouring new wine into old bottles. In truth, he was somewhat distrustful of his new place in the sun. He was afraid of being a fad, the momentary focus of the curiosity of dilettantes, charlatans, and student sociologists. It was common sense for him to attempt to establish himself on something more solid than the theatrical reputation of Florence Mills or the *bizarreries* of what many people thought to be the Greenwich Village influence. New forms were faddish froth: material the marrow. And what more arresting material than the self-revealing truth! . . .

Hugh M. Gloster

Jean Toomer

Toomer's *Cane*—a potpourri of stories, sketches, poetry, and drama—is one of the more significant productions of the Negro

Reprinted from *Negro Voices in American Fiction* (Chapel Hill: The University of North Carolina Press, 1948), pp. 128–30, by permission of the publisher. Copyright © 1948 by the University of North Carolina Press.

Renascence. In this book a colored writer, for possibly the first time in American Negro fiction, handles inflammatory interracial themes without abandonment of the artist's point of view. As Waldo Frank observes:

> For Toomer, the Southland is not a problem to be solved; it is a field of loveliness to be sung: the Georgia Negro is not a downtrodden soul to be uplifted; he is material for gorgeous painting: the segregated self-conscious brown belt of Washington is not a topic to be discussed and exposed; it is a subject of beauty and of drama, worthy of creation in literary form.[1]

Cane is divided into three parts. The first, with rural Georgia as a background, sets forth the tragic lives of women of that section. Karintha inevitably becomes a prostitute. Becky, a wanton white woman, bears two colored sons who, after their mother's lonely death, leave their home town bitterly hated by whites and Negroes. Carma is discovered in marital unfaithfulness. Fern unresponsively submits to lustful men who are baffled and ashamed after selfishly satiating their passions. Esther, near-white daughter of a colored merchant, is strangely attracted to a black religious fanatic. Louisa's Negro admirer slashes her white paramour to death and is subsequently lynched.[2] The chief importance of these stories lies in their departure from the traditional treatment of sex by Negro authors. The candor, shamelessness, and objectivity manifested by Toomer in the presentation of these women caused DuBois to designate him as the "writer who first dared to emancipate the colored world from the conventions of sex." [3]

The second part of *Cane* shifts from the folk life of Georgia to the bourgeois Negro society of Washington. Here again Toomer neither debunks nor glorifies but, as Sterling Brown observes, "pictures Washington with the thoroughness of one who knew it from the inside." [4] "Seventh Street," called "a bastard of Prohibition and the War," is a description of a Washington background. "Avey" reflects the trend away from middle-class conventions by

---

[1] Jean Toomer, *Cane* (New York, 1923), pp. viii–ix. Foreword by Waldo Frank.

[2] "Blood-Burning Moon," the short story in which Louisa is the leading female character, appears in O'Brien's *Best Short Stories of 1923*.

[3] W. E. B. DuBois and Alain Locke, "The Younger Literary Movement," *The Crisis*, XXVII (1924), 161.

[4] Sterling Brown, *The Negro in American Fiction* (Washington, 1937), p. 153.

revealing the affection of a young man for an orphan woman who is "no better than a whore." "Theater," a study of class-consciousness within the Negro group, unfolds the mutual attraction between a chorus girl and the "dictie, educated, stuck-up" brother of the manager of the show. "Box Seat" recounts an ill-fated middle-class romance. "Bona and Paul," having Chicago as a setting, describes the failure of a white girl and a passing mulatto youth to become lovers because of the boy's own race-consciousness and his associates' suspicion of his swarthy complexion. In the stories of the second part of *Cane*, therefore, Toomer shows the Negro facing the problems of caste, respectability, and prejudice in Washington and Chicago.

The third section, returning to rural Georgia, contains one long and occasionally obscure story, "Kabnis," a character study of a learned but excessively emotional Northern Negro teaching in a small town. Sensitive to white oppression and disgusted by Negro inertia, Kabnis resorts to dissipation and is fired by Hanby, the principal of the school. In his characterization of Hanby, Toomer satirizes the dissimulating Negro administrator who poses as a haughty aristocrat among his own people, as an Uncle Tom among Southern whites, and as a staunch Yankee supporter among Bostonians. Another interesting character is Layman, a soft-pedaling teacher-preacher "who has traveled in almost every nook and corner of the state and hence knows more than would be good for anyone other than a silent man." Layman does not believe in disturbing Southern whites:

> "An Mr. Kabnis, kindly remember youre in the land of cotton—hell of a land. Th white folks get th boll; the niggers get th stalk. An dont you dare touch th boll, or even look at it. They'll swing y sho."

Lewis, a purposeful and clear-headed young man, "is what Kabnis might have been," if he had not succumbed to debauchery and despair. Analyzing the character of Kabnis, Lewis says:

> "Life has already told him more than he is capable of knowing. It has given him in excess of what he can receive. I have been offered. Stuff in his stomach curdled, and he vomited me."

Evidently Toomer's implication, as Montgomery Gregory suggests, "is that there must be a welding into one great personality of

Kabnis and Lewis: the great emotionalism of the race guided and directed by a great purpose and super-intelligence." [5]

Cane, being an experimental work in its quest for appropriate literary forms and diction, is debilitated by occasional incoherence, which may have been inspired by Waldo Frank, and undue striving for effect. Munson has noted the architectonic influence of Sherwood Anderson in "Fern" and "Avey" as well as that of Frank in "Theater." [6] All these considerations notwithstanding, *Cane* is noteworthy because of its departure from argumentation and apologetics in the treatment of interracial subject matter as well as because of its prefiguration of Southern realism and Negro self-revelation. As Waldo Frank says:

> It is a harbinger of the South's literary maturity: of its emergence from the obsession put upon its minds by the unending racial crisis —an obsession from which writers have made their indirect escape through sentimentalism, exoticism, polemic, "problem" fiction, and moral melodrama. It marks the dawn of direct and unafraid creation. [7]

---

[5] Montgomery Gregory, Review of *Cane, Opportunity,* I (1923), 375.
[6] Gorham B. Munson, "The Significance of Jean Toomer," *Opportunity,* III (1925), 262.
[7] Toomer, *op. cit.,* p. ix.

Alain Locke

From *Native Son* to *Invisible Man:* A Review of the Literature of the Negro for 1952

In the thirty years' span of my active reviewing experience, there have been in my judgment three points of peak development in

---

Reprinted from *Phylon,* XIV (First Quarter, 1953), 34, by permission of the editor of *Phylon.*

Negro fiction by Negro writers. In 1923 from a relatively low plateau of previous problem fiction, Jean Toomer's *Cane* rose to unprecedented artistic heights. Not only in style but in conception it raised a new summit, as it soared above the plane of propaganda and apologetics to a self-sufficient presentation of Negro life in its own idiom and gave it proud and self-revealing evaluation. More than that, the emotional essences of the Southland were hauntingly evoked in an impressionistic poetic sort of realism; it captured as well some of the more distinctive tone and color of Negro living. Its only shortcomings were that it was a series of character sketches rather than a full length canvas: a succession of vignettes rather than an entire landscape—and that its author chose not to continue. In 1940, Richard Wright's skillful sociological realism turned a hard but brilliant searchlight on Negro urban life in Chicago and outlined the somber tragedy of Bigger Thomas in a well-studied setting of Northside wealth and Southside poverty. Artistically not the equal of the more masterful series of short stories, *Uncle Tom's Children*, that preceded it, *Native Son's* narrative was masterful and its character delineation as skillful as any work of Dreiser's or Farrell's. The book was marred only by Wright's overreliance on the communist ideology with which he encumbered his powerful indictment of society for Bigger, the double pariah of the slum and the color-line. Wright was essentially sound in his alignment of the social forces involved, but erred artistically in the doctrinally propagandist tone which crept into his novel chapter by chapter until the angry, ineffective end. The greater pity it was—and is— that later he disavowed this ideological commitment that cheated him of an all-time classic of American fiction. Despite this, *Native Son* has remained all these intervening years the Negro novelist's strongest bid for fiction of the first magnitude.

But 1952 is the significant year of Ellison's *Invisible Man*, a great novel, although also not without its artistic flaws, sad to say....

Robert A. Bone

Jean Toomer

The writers of the Lost Generation, as John Aldridge has observed, "were engaged in a revolution designed to purge language of the old restraints of the previous century and to fit it to the demands of a younger, more realistic time." [1] Stein and Hemingway in prose, Pound and Eliot in poetry, were threshing and winnowing, testing and experimenting with words, stretching them and refocusing them, until they became the pliant instruments of a new idiom. The only Negro writer of the 1920's who participated on equal terms in the creation of the modern idiom was a young poet-novelist named Jean Toomer.

Jean Toomer's *Cane* (1923) is an important American novel. By far the most impressive product of the Negro Renaissance, it ranks with Richard Wright's *Native Son* and Ralph Ellison's *Invisible Man* as a measure of the Negro novelist's highest achievement. Jean Toomer belongs to that first rank of writers who use words almost as a plastic medium, shaping new meanings from an original and highly personal style. Since stylistic innovation requires great technical dexterity, Toomer displays a concern for technique which is fully two decades in advance of the period. While his contemporaries of the Harlem School were still experimenting with a crude literary realism, Toomer had progressed beyond the naturalistic novel to "the higher realism of the emotions," to symbol, and to myth.

Jean Toomer (1894—) was born in Washington, D.C., where his parents, who were cultivated Negroes of Creole stock, had moved in order to educate their children. Toomer's maternal grandfather, P. B. S. Pinchback, had been acting governor of Louisiana during Reconstruction days, so that tales of slavery and Reconstruction were a household tradition. Toomer was educated for the law at the University of Wisconsin and at the City College of New York, but literature soon became his first love. An avant-garde poet and

---

Reprinted from *The Negro Novel in America* (New Haven: Yale University Press, 1958) pp. 80–89, by permission of the author and the publisher. Copyright © 1958 by Yale University Press.

[1] *After the Lost Generation* (New York and London: McGraw-Hill, 1951), p. 88.

short-story writer, he contributed regularly to such little magazines as *Broom, Secession, Double Dealer, Dial,* and *Little Review.* After a brief literary apprenticeship in cosmopolitan New York, he visited rural Georgia as a country schoolteacher—an experience which directly inspired the production of *Cane.*

During his formative period Toomer was a member of a semi-mystical literary group which included Hart Crane, Waldo Frank, Gorham Munson, and Kenneth Burke. Influenced philosophically by Ouspensky's *Tertium Organum,* they formed a bloc called Art as Vision—some of their catchwords being "the new slope of consciousness," "the superior logic of metaphor," and "noumenal knowledge." The group eventually split over the writings of Gurdjieff, the Russian mystic. So far did Toomer succumb to Gurdjieff's spell that he spent the summer of 1926 at the Gurdjieff Institute in Fontainebleau, France, returning to America to proselytize actively for his mystical philosophy.

In spite of his wide and perhaps primary association with white intellectuals, as an artist Toomer never underestimated the importance of his Negro identity. He attained a universal vision not by ignoring race as a local truth, but by coming face to face with his particular tradition. His pilgrimage to Georgia was a conscious attempt to make contact with his hereditary roots in the Southland. Of Georgia, Toomer wrote: "There one finds soil in the sense that the Russians know it—the soil every art and literature that is to live must be embedded in." [2] This sense of soil is central to *Cane* and to Toomer's artistic vision. "When one is on the soil of one's ancestors," his narrator remarks, "most anything can come to one."

What comes to Toomer, in the first section of *Cane,* is a vision of the parting soul of slavery:

> . . . for though the sun is setting on
> A song-lit race of slaves, it has not set;
> Though late, O soil, it is not too late yet
> To catch thy plaintive soul, leaving, soon gone. [3]

The soul of slavery persists in the "supper-getting-ready songs" of the black women who live on the Dixie Pike—a road which "has grown from a goat path in Africa." It persists in "the soft, listless

---

[2] Quoted in Alain Locke, "Negro Youth Speaks," *The New Negro* (New York: Boni, 1925), p. 51.
[3] *Cane,* p. 21 ("The Song of the Son").

cadence of Georgia's South," in the hovering spirit of a comforting
Jesus, and in the sudden violence of the Georgia moon. It persists
above all in the people, white and black, who have become Ander-
sonian "grotesques" by virtue of their slave inheritance. Part I of
Cane is in fact a kind of Southern *Winesburg, Ohio*. It consists of
the portraits of six women—all primitives—in which an Anderson-
ian narrator mediates between the reader and the author's vision
of life on the Dixie Pike.

There is Karintha, "she who carries beauty" like a pregnancy,
until her perfect beauty and the impatience of young men beget a
fatherless child. Burying her child in a sawdust pile, she takes her
revenge by becoming a prostitute; "the soul of her was a growing
thing ripened too soon."

In "Becky" Toomer dramatizes the South's conspiracy to ignore
miscegenation. Becky is a white woman with two Negro sons. After
the birth of the first, she symbolically disappears from sight into
a cabin constructed by community guilt. After the birth of the
second, she is simply regarded as dead, and no one is surprised
when the chimney of her cabin falls in and buries her. Toward
Becky there is no charity from white or black, but only furtive
attempts to conceal her existence.

Carma's tale, "which is the crudest melodrama," hinges not so
much on marital infidelity as on a childish deception. Accused by
her husband of having other men ("No one blames her for that")
she becomes hysterical, and running into a canebrake, pretends to
shoot herself. "Twice deceived, and the one deception proved the
other." Her husband goes berserk, slashes a neighbor, and is sent
to the chain gang. The tone of the episode is set by the ironic contrast between Carma's apparent strength ("strong as any man")
and her childish behavior.

Fern, whose full name is Fernie May Rosen, combines the suffering of her Jewish father and her Negro mother: "at first sight
of her I felt as if I heard a Jewish cantor sing. . . . As if his singing
rose above the unheard chorus of a folksong." Unable to find fulfillment, left vacant by the bestowal of men's bodies, Fern sits list-
lessly on her porch near the Dixie Pike. Her eyes desire nothing
that man can give her; the Georgia countryside flows into them,
along with something that Toomer's narrator calls God.

"Esther" is a study in sexual repression. The protagonist is a
near-white girl whose father is the richest colored man in town.
Deprived of normal outlets by her social position, she develops a
neurotic life of fantasy which centers upon a virile, black-skinned,

itinerant preacher named King Barlo. At sixteen she imagines herself the mother of his immaculately conceived child. At twenty-seven she tries to translate fantasy into reality by offering herself to Barlo. Rebuffed and humiliated, she retreats into lassitude and frigidity.

Louisa, of "Blood-Burning Moon," has two loves, one white and the other colored. Inflamed by a sexual rivalry deeper than race, they quarrel. One is slashed and the other is lynched. Unlike most Negro writers who have grappled with the subject of lynching, Toomer achieves both form and perspective. He is not primarily concerned with antilynching propaganda, but in capturing a certain atavistic quality in Southern life which defies the restraints of civilized society.

Part II of *Cane* is counterpoint. The scene shifts to Washington, where Seventh Street thrusts a wedge of vitality, brilliance, and movement into the stale, soggy, whitewashed wood of the city. This contrast is an aspect of Toomer's primitivism. The blacks, in his color scheme, represent a full life; the whites, a denial of it. Washington's Negroes have preserved their vitality because of their roots in the rural South, yet whiteness presses in on them from all sides. The "dickty" Negro, and especially the near-white, who are most nearly assimilated to white civilization, bear the brunt of repression and denial, vacillating constantly between two identities. Out of this general frame of reference grow the central symbols of the novel.

Toomer's symbols reflect the profound humanism which forms the base of his philosophical position. Man's essential goodness, he would contend, his sense of brotherhood, and his creative instincts have been crushed and buried by modern industrial society. Toomer's positive values, therefore, are associated with the soil, the cane, and the harvest; with Christian charity, and with giving oneself in love. On the other side of the equation is a series of burial or confinement symbols (houses, alleys, machines, theaters, nightclubs, newspapers) which limit man's growth and act as barriers to his soul. Words are useless in piercing this barrier; Toomer's intellectualizing males are tragic figures because they value talking above feeling. Songs, dreams, dancing, and love itself (being instinctive in nature) may afford access to "the simple beauty of another's soul." The eyes, in particular, are avenues through which we can discover "the truth that people bury in their hearts."

In the second section of *Cane*, Toomer weaves these symbols into a magnificent design, so that his meaning, elusive in any particular episode, emerges with great impact from the whole. "Rhobert" is an attack on the crucial bourgeois value of home ownership: "Rhobert wears a house, like a monstrous diver's helmet, on his head." Like Thoreau's farmer, who traveled through life pushing a barn and a hundred acres before him, Rhobert is a victim of his own property instinct. As he struggles with the weight of the house, he sinks deeper and deeper into the mud:

> Brother, Rhobert is sinking
> Let's open our throats, brother
> Let's sing Deep River when he goes down.

The basic metaphor in "Avey" compares a young girl to the trees planted in boxes along V Street, "the young trees that whinnied like colts impatient to be free." Avey's family wants her to become a school teacher, but her bovine nature causes her to prefer a somewhat older profession. Yet, ironically, it is not she but the narrator who is a failure, who is utterly inadequate in the face of Avey's womanhood.

In "Theatre" Toomer develops his "dickty" theme, through an incident involving a chorus girl and a theater-manager's brother. As John watches a rehearsal, he is impressed by Dorris' spontaneity, in contrast to the contrived movements of the other girls. He momentarily contemplates an affair, but reservations born of social distance prevent him from consummating his desire, except in a dream. Dorris, who hopes fleetingly for home and children from such a man, is left at the end of the episode with only the sordid reality of the theater.

"Calling Jesus" plays a more important role than its length would indicate in unifying the symbolism of the novel. It concerns a woman, urbanized and spiritually intimidated, whose "soul is like a little thrust-tailed dog that follows her, whimpering." At night, when she goes to sleep in her big house, the little dog is left to shiver in the vestibule. "Some one ... eoho Jesus ... soft as the bare feet of Christ moving across bales of Southern cotton, will steal in and cover it that it need not shiver, and carry it to her where she sleeps, cradled in dream-fluted cane."

In "Box Seat" Toomer comes closest to realizing his central theme. The episode opens with an invocation: "Houses are shy girls whose eyes shine reticently upon the dusk body of the street. Upon the gleaming limbs and asphalt torso of a dreaming nigger. Shake your curled wool-blossoms, nigger. Open your liver-lips to the lean white spring. Stir the root-life of a withered people. Call them from their houses and teach them to dream" (p. 104).

The thought is that of a young man, whose symbolic role is developed at once: "I am Dan Moore. I was born in a canefield. The hands of Jesus touched me. I am come to a sick world to heal it." Dan, moreover, comes as a representative of "powerful underground races": "The next world-savior is coming up that way. Coming up. A continent sinks down. The new-world Christ will need consummate skill to walk upon the waters where huge bubbles burst." The redemption motif is echoed in Dan's communion with the old slave: "I asked him if he knew what that rumbling is that comes up from the ground." It is picked up again through the portly Negro woman who sits beside Dan in the theater: "A soil-soaked fragrance comes from her. Through the cement floor her strong roots sink down . . . and disappear in blood-lines that waver south."

The feminine lead is played by Muriel, a school teacher inclined toward conventionality. Her landlady, Mrs. Pribby, is constantly with her, being in essence a projection of Muriel's social fears. The box seat which she occupies at the theater, where her every movement is under observation, renders her relationship to society perfectly. Her values are revealed in her query to Dan, "Why don't you get a good job and settle down?" On these terms only can she love him; meanwhile she avoids his company by going to a vaudeville performance with a girl friend.

Dan, a slave to "her still unconquered animalism," follows and watches her from the audience. The main attraction consists of a prize fight between two dwarfs for the "heavy-weight championship"; it symbolizes the ultimate degradation of which a false and shoddy culture is capable. Sparring grotesquely, pounding and bruising each other, the dwarfs suggest the traditional clown symbol of modern art. At the climax of the episode the winner presents a blood-spattered rose to Muriel, who recoils, hesitates, and finally submits. The dwarf's eyes are pleading: "Do not shrink. Do not be afraid of me." Overcome with disgust for Muriel's hypocrisy, Dan completes the dwarf's thought from the audience, rising to shout: "JESUS WAS ONCE A LEPER!" Rushing from the theater, he is free at last of his love for Muriel—free, but at the same time sterile: "He is as cool as a green stem that has just shed its flower."

Coming as an anticlimax after "Box Seat," "Bona and Paul" describes an abortive love affair between two Southern students at the University of Chicago—a white girl and a mulatto boy who is "passing." The main tension, reminiscent of Gertrude Stein's

Melanctha, is between knowing and loving, set in the framework of
Paul's double identity. It is not his race consciousness which ter-
minates the relationship, as one critic has suggested, but precisely
his "whiteness," his desire for knowledge, his philosophical bent.
If he had been able to assert his Negro self—that which attracted
Bona to him in the first place—he might have held her love.

In "Kabnis" rural Georgia once more provides a setting. This is
the long episode which comprises the concluding section of *Cane.*
By now the symbolic values of Toomer's main characters can be
readily assessed. Ralph Kabnis, the protagonist, is a school teacher
from the North who cringes in the face of his tradition. A spiritual
coward, he cannot contain "the pain and beauty of the South";
cannot embrace the suffering of the past, symbolized by slavery;
cannot come to terms with his own bastardy; cannot master his
pathological fear of being lynched. Consumed with self-hatred and
cut off from any organic connection with the past, he resembles
nothing so much as a scarecrow: "Kabnis, a promise of soil-soaked
beauty; uprooted, thinning out. Suspended a few feet above the
soil whose touch would resurrect him."

Lewis, by way of contrast, is a Christ figure, an extension of Dan
Moore. Almost a T. S. Eliot creation ("I'm on a sort of contract
with myself"), his function is to shock others into moral awareness. It is Lewis who confronts Kabnis with his moral cowardice:
"Can't hold them, can you? Master; slave. Soil; and the over-
arching heavens. Dusk; dawn. They fight and bastardize you. The
sun tint of your cheeks, flame of the great season's multi-colored
leaves, tarnished, burned. Split, shredded, easily burned" (p. 218).

Halsey, unlike Kabnis, has not been crushed by Southern life,
but absorbed into it. Nevertheless, his spiritual degradation is
equally thorough. An artisan and small shopkeeper like his father
before him, he "belongs" in a sense that Kabnis does not. Yet in
order to maintain his place in the community, he must submit to
the indignities of Negro life in the South. Like Booker T. Washington, whose point of view he represents, Halsey has settled for
something less than manhood. Restless, groping tentatively toward
Lewis, he escapes from himself through his craft, and through an
occasional debauch with the town prostitute, whom he loved as a
youth.

Father John, the old man who lives beneath Halsey's shop, represents a link with the Negro's ancestral past. Concealed by the
present generation as an unpleasant memory, the old man is thrust
into a cellar which resembles the hold of a slave ship. There he sits,

"A mute John the Baptist of a new religion, or a tongue-tied shadow of an old." When he finally speaks, it is to rebuke the white folks for the sin of slavery. The contrast between Lewis and Kabnis is sharpened by their respective reactions to Father John. Through the old slave, Lewis is able to "merge with his source," but Kabnis can only deny: "An' besides, he aint my past. My ancestors were Southern blue-bloods."

In terms of its dramatic movement "Kabnis" is a steep slope downward,[4] approximating the progressive deterioration of the protagonist. Early in the episode Kabnis is reduced to a scarecrow replica of himself by his irrational fears. His failure to stand up to Hanby, an authoritarian school principal, marks a decisive loss in his power of self-direction. Gradually he slips into a childlike dependence, first on Halsey, then on the two prostitutes, and finally on Halsey's little sister, Carrie Kate. In the course of the drunken debauch with which the novel ends, Kabnis becomes a clown, without dignity or manhood, wallowing in the mire of his own self-hatred. The stark tragedy of "Kabnis" is relieved only by the figure of Carrie Kate, the unspoiled child of a new generation, who may yet be redeemed through her ties with Father John.

A critical analysis of *Cane* is a frustrating task, for Toomer's art, in which "outlines are reduced to essences," is largely destroyed in the process of restoration. No paraphrase can properly convey the aesthetic pleasure derived from a sensitive reading of *Cane*. Yet in spite of Toomer's successful experiment with the modern idiom— or perhaps because of it—*Cane* met with a cold reception from the public, hardly selling 500 copies during its first year. This poor showing must have been a great disappointment to Toomer, and undoubtedly it was a chief cause of his virtual retirement from literature. Perhaps in his heart of hearts Jean Toomer found it singularly appropriate that the modern world should bury *Cane*. Let us in any event delay the exhumation no longer.

---

[4] See Gorham B. Munson, *Destinations* (New York: 1928), pp. 178–96.

S. P. Fullenwider

Jean Toomer: Lost Generation, or Negro Renaissance

Now that the Jean Toomer papers have found a home at the Fisk University Library it is no longer necessary to speculate as to why Toomer ceased to write after he published *Cane* in 1923. In fact, he did not cease to write. He continued to write, and write voluminously; but to no avail—he could find no publisher. The story of Toomer's literary efforts after 1923 is a story of frustration, despair and failure—this after what was surely one of the most promising beginnings in the history of American literature. Toomer's story is one of a young man caught up in the tangled skein of race relations in America. But it goes beyond even that. For a time, at least, it was the story of modern man; the story of a search for identity—for an absolute in a world that had dissolved into flux. It is a story of success—at the age of thirty-one his search for an identity-giving absolute was over. It is a story of tragedy. As long as he was searching he was a fine creative artist; when the search ended, so did his creative powers. So long as he was searching, his work was the cry of one caught in the modern human condition; it expressed modern man's lostness, his isolation. Once Toomer found an identity-giving absolute, his voice ceased to be the cry of modern man and became the voice of the schoolmaster complacently pointing out the way—his way. It now seems possible to take a few hesitant steps toward a closer understanding of the Negro American literary tradition by asking the question: "Who was Jean Toomer?"

Toomer's overriding concern for the human condition grew out of an early lack of self-esteem, a concomitant tendency towards introspection and soul-searching, and a loss of his childhood absolutes. His problem with self-esteem was a product of his early family life, particularly, his relationship with an imperious grandfather, P. B. S. Pinchback. The former Reconstruction lieutenant governor of Louisiana had suffered political and financial reverses when the

Reprinted from *Phylon,* XXVII (Fourth Quarter, 1966), 396–403, by permission of the editor of *Phylon.*

Republicans lost power in the South, and had removed to an impos-
ing house on Washington's Bacon Street, an all white neighborhood. There Pinchback lived a high life—the life of a social lion—
while his prestige lasted. But a politician out of office quickly loses
status and influence. As his fortunes declined, Pinchback became
increasingly autocratic toward his daughter Nina and his sons. The
beautiful Nina married twice, first to a young Southern planter
who disappeared after a year, and then to a ne'er-do-well who mis-
represented his wealth. The second marriage, with its drudgery and
lack of love, killed her. So Jean, a product of the first match, led
a troubled young life with his grandfather.[1]

As Jean Toomer grew in childhood he turned in upon himself,
away from the tyrannical grandfather, away from his unhappy
mother. Slowly he created a rich inner life, but it was a life almost
totally disassociated from the outside world.[2] Pinchback's fortunes
continued to decline. One day he moved the family from Bacon
Street with its white neighborhood to a house on Florida Avenue,
the heart of the Negro upper-class world. Looking back, Toomer
wrote, "With this world—an aristocracy—such as never existed before and perhaps will never exist again in America—mid-way between the white and Negro worlds. For the first time I lived in a
colored world." Toomer liked his new life. He felt that he found
here, "more emotion, more rhythm, more color, more gaiety," [3]
than he had met in the chilling atmosphere of white society. But
this was a time, too, of morbid introspection. Now fourteen, he became a nuisance in the classroom, an inveterate troublemaker. He
became the victim of overpowering sex impulses, and seems to
have concluded that these impulses were destroying his health. He
turned to barbells and special diets. By then the Pinchbacks were
on the verge of poverty and family relations were deteriorating. A
three-year period of revolt and wandering began for the boy. His
revolt first took him to the University of Wisconsin to study agriculture (this lasted a semester), then back to Washington to endure hard looks of reproach. He was assailed by self-doubt. He tried
the Massachusetts College of Agriculture for almost a week, then
a physical training college in Chicago. There he paid more atten-
tion to lectures at the Loop than to physical education. Men like

---

[1] Jean Toomer, "Book of Parents" (Unpublished MS., ca. 1934), pp. 17–37.
Toomer papers, Fisk University Library.
[2] Jean Toomer, "Outline of Autobiography" (Unpublished MS., ca. 1934),
p. 2. Toomer papers, Fisk University Library.
[3] *Ibid.,* p. 8.

Clarence Darrow held forth there on exciting subjects like Darwinism and the ideas of Haeckel—and atheism. Toomer felt his intellectual world collapse. His belief in God, he thought, evaporated. He felt "condemned and betrayed." "In truth," he later wrote, "I did not want to live." [4] His old absolutes were gone; he began a desperate search for new ones. For a time socialism seemed to serve the need.

> I had been, I suppose, unconsciously seeking—as man must ever seek—an intelligible scheme of things, a sort of whole into which everything fit . . . it was the *body*, the *scheme*, the order and inclusion. These evoked and promised to satisfy all in me that had been groping for order from amid the disorder and chaos of my personal experiences. [5]

After Chicago there were further wanderings, further soul-searchings. A reading of Lester F. Ward's *Dynamic Sociology* led to a short fraternization with that subject at New York University. But he found a history course at City College more attractive. Then history became a bore and psychology took its place. World War I came to America and he was rejected by the draft. He tried odd jobs for a year: he sold Fords in Chicago, taught physical education in Milwaukee, and did a ten-day stint as a ship-fitter in a New Jersey shipyard. His contact with the construction workers there caused him to lose interest in socialism. In 1920, Toomer returned, defeated, to his grandfather in Washington. It was not a cheerful reunion. In a mood of bitterness and an atmosphere of rejection he turned to reading literature—Robert Frost, Sherwood Anderson, the imagists. He wrote incessantly, hour upon hour for month after month, tearing up what he wrote. He learned to handle words, learned their symbolic potential. He became an artist. [6]

Toomer learned as he handled words that they had no meaning beyond what he gave them arbitrarily. He began to see that words are mere symbols of things and not the things themselves. [7] He was traveling the road to nominalism, and as he traveled that road he felt the concrete world begin to dissolve about him. He was entering the world of modern alienated man. Apparently it was during

---

[4] *Ibid.*, p. 26.
[5] *Ibid.*, handwritten note on reverse of p. 25.
[6] *Ibid.*, pp. 27–55.
[7] Jean Toomer, "Essentials: Prose and Poems" (Unpublished MS., 1930), pp. 70, 112–18. Toomer papers, Fisk University Library.

this period that he began to experience the severing of his intellect from his emotions—the seemingly peculiar phenomenon of the modern mind that has been described as the "frigidization of the self." The phenomenon has been described as an overwhelming sense of self-consciousness—a standing outside oneself, as it were; an objectification of the self. The intellect seems to overpower the emotions, making it impossible to have effective emotional relations with other people. One finds an impenetrable wall standing between oneself and those one would love.[8] Toomer made the solution of this problem—this "frigidization of the self"—his major intellectual theme. Again and again in his later writings he reverted to his argument that the intellect must somehow be fused with the emotions: "Themosense (thought *and* emotion *and* sensing) is the inner synthesis of functions, which represents the entire individual and gives rise to complete action." [9] Of course, in Toomer's case much of this "frigidization of the self" can be traced to his deliberate retreat from an outside world (his family life) that was too threatening—a retreat into the isolation of subjectivity. In one place he tells of wrongs being inflicted upon him in such profusion that "Finally we reached the stage where we vowed to suffer no more. Of people, of life, of the world we said, 'Don't touch me.' We resolved that no one ever would." [10] It was while in this mood that he accepted an offer in 1921 to act as temporary superintendent of a small Negro industrial school in rural Georgia.

Georgia was for Toomer a small shack in the hills. It was the whispering pines. It was the folk-singing that drifted over in the evenings from the Negro dwellings. Most of all, it was the Southern Negro spirit—a spirit with which he developed a deep feeling of kinship. *Cane* was at once the joy of discovering this folk-spirit and the sadness of the realization that it was a passing thing.

He wrote of the spirituals, "But I learned

> that the Negroes of the town objected to them. They called them 'shouting.' They had victrolas and player-pianos. So, I realized with deep regret, that the spirituals, meeting ridicule, would be certain to die out. With Negroes also the trend was towards the small

---

[8] Walter H. Sokel, *The Writer in Extremis: Expressionism in Twentieth-Century German Literature* (Stanford, 1959), pp. 85–118.
[9] Jean Toomer, *Work-Ideas* I, Mill House Pamphlets. Psychological Series, No. 2 (Doylestown, Pennsylvania, 1937), p. 13.
[10] Jean Toomer, *Living Is Developing,* Mill House Pamphlets, Psychological Series, No. 1 (Doylestown, Pennsylvania, 1937), p. 14.

town and towards the city—and industry and commerce and the machines. The folk-spirit was walking in to die on the modern desert. That spirit was so beautiful. Its death was so tragic." [11]

Toomer, suffering intensely from "frigidization of the self," appears to have entertained the idea that in the Southern Negro folk-spirit he might find emotional release—that in this spirit he might find not only his own salvation but salvation for the modern industrial world. This, at least, is the message of "Box Seat," one of the more substantial of *Cane's* prose-pictures. In it appears Dan, a Southern Negro with a redemptive mission. The setting of "Box Seat" is Washington, D.C., or, in other words, the large city. There one is crushed and shorn of spirit by the heavy hand of civilization.

Houses are shy girls whose eyes shine reticently upon the dusk body of the street. Upon the gleaming limbs and asphalt torso of a dreaming nigger. Shake your curled wool-blossoms, nigger. Open your liver lips to the lean white spring. Stir the root-life of a withered people. Call them from their houses, and teach them to dream.

Dan, hot-blooded and virile, is up from the primitive regions of the South to restore vigor and passion to a jaded, over-civilized people —people conquered by "zoo-restrictions and keeper-taboos." "I am Dan More," he says, "I was born in a cane-field. The hands of Jesus touched me. I am come to a sick world to heal it." [12]

To Toomer's mind the plight of modern man is that industrial civilization has shorn him of emotional spontaneity—has made him the passive mechanical pawn of social forces. While living in the hills of Georgia, Toomer could almost believe the answer lay with Dan. During those months Toomer must have felt a closer identification with the Negro race than he had ever felt before, or was to feel thereafter. A year later, in mid-1922, he wrote of his feelings to the editor of the *Liberator:* "Within the last two or three years, however, my growing need for artistic expression has pulled me deeper and deeper into the Negro group. . . . I found myself loving it in a way that I could never love the other." [13] There is every rea-

---

[11] Toomer, "Autobiography," *op. cit.*, pp. 58–59.
[12] Jean Toomer, "Box Seat," *Cane* (New York, 1923), pp. 104–29.
[13] Jean Toomer to editor of *Liberator,* August 19, 1922. Toomer papers, Fisk University Library.

son to believe that this was a sincere statement; Toomer, after all, had been searching for an identity throughout most of his life. But there is good evidence that Toomer was not secure in his new-found faith, even while in the midst of composing *Cane*. In "Kabnis," the final and most compelling sketch of the book, he put on record his doubts concerning the Negro race in America. Kabnis, a product of white men's Christianity, a slave religion, is portrayed as a weak and groveling character who projects his self-hatred outward against an ex-slave, blind and deaf from years of toil. In Kabnis' eyes the old man is a servile product of the Christian religion—an Uncle Tom. A much stronger character in the sketch, Lewis, saw in the old man something much different. He saw strength growing out of hardship and pain. Thus, Toomer had two points of view towards Negroes: one expressing his doubts, one expressing his hope; one repelling him, the other attracting him. The significant point is that neither point of view gained the ascendancy in "Kabnis."

Thus, for a period of perhaps a year or two, the period during which he composed *Cane*, Toomer found a new identity-giving absolute in the Negro folk-spirit. But the absolute had, at best, a tenuous hold on the poet. It proved no more enduring than those that had gone before. Shortly after the publication of *Cane*, Toomer again felt himself immersed in chaos and doubt: "Everything was in chaos. I saw this chaos clearly, I could and did describe and analyze its factors so well that I got a reputation for being a sort of genius of chaos." [14]

What happened to Toomer in the years between 1923 and 1925 is described by Gorham Munson, who knew him well at the time. Toomer continued his quest for what Munson calls "unity," or "personal wholeness," first by training his "conscious control of the body," and then by spending the summer of 1924 at the Gurdjieff Institute, Fontainebleau, France. [15] Toomer found what he was looking for in Gurdjieff's philosophy—an interesting blend of Freudian categories and religion—became a disciple and spent many of his summers in Fontainebleau, returning each fall to organize psychological experiments in the United States. But the crucial moment for Toomer came one summer evening in 1926. It happened at the end of one of those humdrum days of no special

---

[14] Toomer, "Autobiography," *op. cit.*, p. 63.
[15] Gorham B. Munson, "The Significance of Jean Toomer," *Opportunity*, III (September, 1925), 262–63.

significance. Toomer was waiting on an El platform in New York City, when suddenly, as he says, he transcended himself: "I was born above the body into a world of psychological reality. . . . In my private language I shall call this experience the Second Conception." [16]

That was it for Toomer; he had his absolute; his search was over. From that time he began to proselytize in the age-old tradition of missionaries. He wrote novels, he wrote philosophic works, he wrote descriptions of psychological experiments,[17] and he wrote volumes of material that is unclassifiable—all with the purpose of persuasion. The publishers were not buying; his literary life after 1926 became a dreary round of rejection slips. The fault was not his nor his publishers'. He had come up with an answer to the troubles that plagued the age. He had an answer for Van Wyck Brook's cry of "externalization"; for Waldo Frank's plight of being "objectified." He had found an answer for modern man's agonizing sense of incompleteness. His answer was couched disconcertingly in half-psychological, half-mystical language ("Our center of gravity is displaced. Our essence is passive; and we lack essential self-activating energies. . . . We have no being-aims and purposes."),[18] but what he was doing, in essence, was putting into his own symbols the age-old experience of religious conversion. Following willy-nilly behind Gurdjieff, he had got himself completely at cross-purposes with the whole thrust of American intelligence of the 1920's. Van Wyck Brooks, Charles S. Johnson, Alain Locke—all were asking that man, through his creative art, turn to experience. The answer found by these modern critics lay in creating beauty and meaning out of the living contact with the world of reality. Toomer was saying just the opposite: turn for beauty and meaning to your inner essence. "An artist," he wrote, "is able, by effort to contact his own essence, wherein exist common universal symbols." [19] Toomer was asking his age to adopt another absolute. The age was not buying.

Toomer's artistic expression lost something once he had found

---

[16] Jean Toomer, "From Exile into Being" (Unpublished MS., 1938), p. 1 of Prescript. Toomer papers, Fisk University Library.
[17] See, for example, Jean Toomer (Unpublished MSS. of novels: "The Gallonwerps," ca. 1927; "York Beach," ca. 1928; "Transatlantic Crossing," ca. 1930; "Eight-Day World," ca. 1932; Unpublished MS. of a philosophic work, "Essentials: Definitions and Aphroisms," 1931; Unpublished MS. of a psychological experiment, "Portage Potential," 1931). Toomer papers, Fisk University Library.
[18] Toomer, "Essentials: Prose and Poems," *op. cit.,* p. 63.
[19] *Ibid.,* p. 46.

his answer—it became didactic, it became unconvincing. His unpublished novel, "Eight-Day World" (c. 1932) is a case in point.
It pictures a group of people aboard a transatlantic liner escaping
from their unsatisfactory lives in America. The critique of life in
America was the one expressed by a hundred writers in the 1920's.
Life had become materialistic, commercial, and unfulfilling. The
group escaping from this life aboard the liner was no sooner at sea
than in-fighting and back-biting began. The people felt inadequate
to themselves, and yet strove for independence from others. It was
Toomer's early experience being retold. Hugh was the one man of
the story who understood something of what was going on, but he
was in the same predicament as the others, trying to break down
the barriers his own inadequacy built up between him and them,
trying, without success, to find fulfillment. Finally, Hugh found his
fulfillment in the beautiful Vera, and at the same time crystallized
a philosophy of it all. He had come to understand that each person
must attain a satisfying independence and yet give of self. That is
the goal. But in order to achieve it, one must transcend oneself:
"This means," said Hugh, "that we must recapture our full *being.
Being* is the base of everything." [20]

"Eight-Day World" ended as Toomer had ended, with all problems solved, with everyone satisfied. The artist could no longer express modern man's restlessness and lostness. His work had become
smug—and dead. Toomer had been modern in *Cane*. There the
author had confronted his readers with the pain of reality unmiti-
gated by the pleasant knowledge of having in hand The Answer.
After writing *Cane*, Toomer fled from reality, found his absolute
and clung to it. He talked about finding "being," but he would have
been horrified at the modern definition of being—the "being" of
Heidigger or of Sartre. He turned from experience of outward reality to an inner thing he called "essence" or "being," thinking that
the thing he was camouflaging with the symbols of psychology was
newly discovered. By 1940 he realized it was not new. He requested
admittance to the Society of Friends, saying: "For some time we
have shared the fundamental faith of the Friends. . . ." [21] His "essence" had been none other than the Quakers' "inner light"; in his
1926 experience of "Second Conception" had been the experience
of religious conversion. Toomer had gone full cycle from his child-

---

[20] Toomer, "Eight-Day World," *op. cit.,* pp. 324–25.
[21] Jean Toomer to Overseers, Buckingham Meeting (Lahaska, Pennsylvania,
August 28, 1940). Toomer papers, Fisk University Library.

hood faith in God, through total rejection in *Cane*, and then back again to God.

What, then, shall we say about Jean Toomer? Does he stand within the Negro American literary tradition? The question is not an easy one, and the answer must be a much more arbitrary one than has always been assumed. In none of his literary efforts subsequent to *Cane* did he make race a central or even important issue. Beyond that, he made some positive efforts to disassociate his name from Negro literature. When, for example, James Weldon Johnson, in 1930, asked his permission to use some of the poetry from *Cane* in the revised edition of *The Book of American Negro Poetry*, Toomer replied in the negative, saying,

> My poems are not Negro poems, nor are they Anglo-Saxon or white or English poems. My prose likewise. They are, first, mine. And, second, in so far as general race or stock is concerned, they spring from the result of racial blending here in America which has produced a new race or stock. We may call this stock the American stock or race. . . .[22]

Evidently the division of mankind into categories of race was not one of Toomer's preoccupations after his 1926 conversion experience—he had found his identity in religion and not race. Before 1926 he had made one serious attempt to find the answer to his emotional needs through an identification with the Negro race. The result had been *Cane*. I suspect that *Cane* should be seen as the point at which the broad current represented by the aspirations and needs of the Lost Generation touched the current of Negro social protest, leaving a minor monument to both.

---

[22] Jean Toomer to James Weldon Johnson, July 11, 1930. Toomer papers, Fisk University Library.

Arna Bontemps

The Negro Renaissance: Jean Toomer and the Harlem Writers of the 1920's

That story from one of the old countries about the man with the marriageable daughter comes to mind when I think of a leading literary pundit in the second decade of this century. In a land where brides were bartered it was, of course, not uncommon for subtle salesmanship to flourish. Sometimes it could become high pressured. In this old yarn the eager parent of the bride had recited so many of his daughter's excellent qualities the prospective husband began to wonder whether she had any human faults at all. "Well, yes," the father finally acknowledged. "A tiny one. She is just a little bit pregnant."

Similarly, in the Twenties the man whose comments on writing by or about Negroes were most respected was just a little bit Negro. He was William Stanley Braithwaite, literary critic for the Boston *Transcript* and editor of an annual series, "Anthologies of Magazine Verse, 1913–1929." In "Braithwaite's Anthologies," as they were commonly known, Spoon River poems by Edgar Lee Masters, chants by Vachel Lindsay, free verse by Carl Sandburg and the early works of many other important American poets were recognized and published before the authors had received general acceptance or acclaim.

But Braithwaite did not completely disassociate himself from Negroes, as he might have. Indeed, he was awarded the Spingarn medal in 1917 as "the Negro who, according to a committee appointed by the board [of the NAACP], has reached the highest achievement in his field of activity." His occasional observations on Negro writing in the decade preceding Harlem's golden era are therefore useful as prologue. In 1913, for example, Braithwaite took note of James Weldon Johnson's "Fiftieth Anniversary Ode" on the Emancipation and suggested that it represented a move by

Reprinted from *Anger and Beyond,* edited by Herbert Hill (New York: Harper & Row, Publishers, 1966), pp. 20–36, by permission of the publisher. Copyright © 1966 by Herbert Hill.

the Negro poet to disengage himself. A decade of near silence had followed Paul Laurence Dunbar's last lyrics, and Braithwaite's language created an image of the Negro poet in chains, seeking to free himself.

The reappearance of this Johnson poem in a collection called *Fifty Years and Other Poems*, in 1917—the same year that Braithwaite was awarded the Spingarn medal, incidentally—prompted Braithwaite to remark, in effect, that this could be the beginning of something big, like a new awakening among Negro writers, perhaps. But, actually, Johnson's most significant poetic achievement was still a decade in the future, when his collection of folk sermons in verse was to be published as *God's Trombones* in 1927. Nevertheless, Braithwaite appears to have picked the right year for the first sign of "disengagement" or "awakening" or whatever it was. The year 1917 now stands out, where Negro poetry in the United States is concerned, as the year in which Claude McKay's poem "The Harlem Dancer" appeared in *The Seven Arts* magazine under the pen name of Eli Edwards. You may know the poem. It was in sonnet form:

> Applauding youths laughed with young prostitutes
> And watched her perfect, half-clothed body sway;
> Her voice was like the sound of blended flutes
> Blown by black players upon a picnic day.
> She sang and danced on gracefully and calm,
> The light gauze hanging loose about her form;
> To me she seemed a proudly-swaying palm
> Grown lovelier for passing through a storm.
> Upon her swarthy neck black shiny curls
> Luxuriant fell; and tossing coins in praise,
> The wine-flushed, bold-eyed boys, and even the girls,
> Devoured her shape with eager, passionate gaze;
> But looking at her falsely-smiling face,
> I knew her self was not in that strange place.

Now this I submit was the anticipation and the theme of an early outburst of creativity later described as the Negro or Harlem Renaissance. When McKay's "The Harlem Dancer" reappeared in his collection *Harlem Shadows* in 1922, along with other poems so fragrant and fresh they almost drugged the senses, things immediately began to happen. Here was poetry written from experience, differing from poetry written from books and other cultural media in somewhat the same way that real flowers differ from artificial ones. A chorus of other new voices led by Jean Toomer, Langston Hughes and Countee Cullen promptly began to make the Twenties a decade which *Time* magazine has described as Harlem's "golden age."

Interestingly, Braithwaite recognized McKay as the first voice in this new chorus, but he spoke of him as "a genius meshed in [a] dilemma." It bothered Braithwaite that McKay seemed to "waver between the racial and the universal notes." In some of his poems, Braithwaite felt, McKay was clearly "contemplating life and nature with a wistful sympathetic passion," but in others the poet became what Braithwaite called a "strident propagandist, using his poetic gifts to clothe arrogant and defiant thoughts." Braithwaite thought this was bad. He cited McKay's "The Harlem Dancer" and his "Spring in New Hampshire" as instances of the former, his "If We Must Die" as a shameless instance of the latter. But, ironically, a generation later it was "If We Must Die," a poem that would undoubtedly stir the blood of almost any Black Muslim, that Sir Winston Churchill quoted as climax and conclusion of his oration before the joint houses of the American Congress when he was seeking to draw this nation into the common effort in World War II. McKay had written it as the Negro American's defiant answer to lynching and mob violence in the Southern states. Churchill made it the voice of the embattled Allies as he read aloud McKay's poem "If We Must Die."

Obviously neither Churchill nor McKay had at that time considered the possibilities of nonviolence. The poem does show, however, how a short span of years and certain historical developments can alter the meaning of a literary work. It also demonstrates the risk of trying to separate too soon the local or special subject from the universal.

But if Braithwaite's attitude toward Claude McKay was ambivalent, it was certainly unequivocal with respect to the second, and in some ways the most inspiring, of the writers who made the Harlem Renaissance significant in the long-range development of the Negro writer in the United States.

"In Jean Toomer, the author of *Cane*," Braithwaite wrote in 1925, "we come upon the very first artist of the race, who with all an artist's passion and sympathy for life, its hurts, its sympathies, its desires, its joys, its defeats and strange yearnings, can write about the Negro without the surrender or compromise of the artist's vision. So objective is it, that we feel that it is a mere accident that birth or association has thrown him into contact with

the life he has written about. He would write just as well, just as
poignantly, just as transmutingly, about the peasants of Russia,
or the peasants of Ireland, had experience brought him in touch
with their existence. *Cane* is a book of gold and bronze, of dusk and
flame, of ecstasy and pain, and Jean Toomer is a bright morning
star of a new day of the race in literature."

Cane was published in 1923 after portions of it had first appeared in *Broom, The Crisis, Double Dealer, Liberator, Little
Review, Modern Review, Nomad, Prairie* and *S 4 N*. But *Cane*
and Jean Toomer, its gifted author, presented an enigma—an
enigma which has, if anything, deepened in the forty-three years
since its publication. Given such a problem, perhaps one may be
excused for not wishing to separate the man from his work. Indeed, so separated, Toomer's writing could scarcely be understood
at all, and its significance would escape us now as it has escaped
so many others in the past.

In any case, *Who's Who in Colored America* listed Toomer in
1927 and gave the following vita:

> b. Dec. 26, 1894, Washington, D.C.; s. Nathan and Nina (Pinch-
> back) Toomer; educ. Public Scho., Washington, D.C.; Dunbar,
> High Scho.; Univ. of Wisconsin, 1914–15; taught schools, Sparta,
> Ga., for four months, traveled, worked numerous occupations; auth.
> *Cane,* pub. Boni and Liveright, 1923; Short Stories and Literary
> Criticisms in various magazines; address, c/o Civic Club, 439 W.
> 23rd St., New York, N.Y.

Needless to say, no subsequent listing of Toomer is to be found
in this or any other directory of conspicuous Negro Americans.
Judging by the above, however, Toomer had always been elusive,
and the interest that *Cane* awakened did nothing to change this.
Several years later Toomer faded completely into white obscurity
leaving behind a literary mystery almost as intriguing as the dis-
appearance of Ambrose Bierce into Mexico in 1913.

Why did he do it? What did it mean?

Concerned with writing, as we are, we automatically turn to
Toomer's book for clues. This could be difficult, because copies
are scarce. *Cane*'s two printings were small, and the few people
who went quietly mad about the strange book were evidently unable to do much toward enlarging its audience. But among these
few was practically the whole generation of young Negro writers
then just beginning to appear, and their reaction to Toomer's *Cane*

marked an awakening that soon thereafter began to be called a Negro renaissance.

Cane's influence was not limited to the happy band that included Langston Hughes, Countee Cullen, Eric Walrond, Zora Neale Hurston, Wallace Thurman, Rudolph Fisher and their contemporaries of the Twenties. Subsequent writing by Negroes in the United States as well as in the West Indies and Africa has continued to reflect its mood and often its method, and, one feels, it also has influenced the writing about Negroes by others. And certainly no earlier volume of poetry or fiction or both had come close to expressing the ethos of the Negro in the Southern setting as *Cane* did.

There are many odd and provocative things about *Cane*, and not the least is its form. Reviewers who read it in 1923 were generally stumped. Poetry and prose were whipped together in a kind of frappé. Realism was mixed with what they called mysticism, and the result seemed to many of them confusing. Still, one of them could conclude that *"Cane* is an interesting, occasionally beautiful and often queer book of exploration into old country and new ways of writing." Another noted, "Toomer has not interviewed the Negro, has not asked opinions about him, has not drawn conclusions about him from his reactions to outside stimuli, but has made the much more searching, and much more self-forgetting effort of seeing life with him, through him."

Such comment was cautious, however, compared to the trumpetings of Waldo Frank in the Foreword he contributed:

A poet has arisen among our American youth who has known how to turn the essence and materials of his Southland into the essences and materials of literature. A poet has arisen in that land who writes, not as a Southerner, not as a rebel against Southerners, not as a Negro, not as apologist or priest or critic: who writes as a *poet*. The fashioning of beauty is ever foremost in his inspiration: not forcedly but simply, and because these ultimate aspects of his world are to him more real than all its specific problems. He has made songs and lovely stories of his land. . . .

The gifted Negro has been too often thwarted from becoming a poet because his world was forever forcing him to recollect that he was a Negro. The artist must lose such lesser identities in the great well of life. . . . The whole will and mind of the creator must go below the surfaces of race. And this has been an almost impossible condition for the American Negro to achieve, forced every moment of his life into a specific and superficial plane of consciousness. . . .

It seems to me, therefore, that this is a first book in more ways than one. It is a harbinger of the South's literary maturity: of its emergence from the obsession put upon its minds by the unending racial crisis. . . . It marks the dawn of direct and unafraid creation. And, as the initial work of a man of twenty-seven, it is the harbinger of a literary force of whose incalculable future I believe no reader of this book will doubt.

It is well to keep in mind the time of these remarks. Of the novels by which T. S. Stribling is remembered, only *Birthright* had been published. Julia Peterkin had not yet published a book. DuBose Heyward's *Porgy* was still two years away. William Faulkner's first novel was three years away. His Mississippi novels were six or more years in the future. Robert Penn Warren, a student at Vanderbilt University, was just beginning his association with the Fugitive poets. His first novel was still more than a decade and a half ahead. Tennessee Williams was just nine years old.

A chronology of Negro writers is equally revealing. James Weldon Johnson had written lyrics for popular songs, some of them minstrel style, and a sort of documentary novel obscurely published under a pseudonym, but *God's Trombones* was a good four years in the offing. Countee Cullen's *Color* was two and Langston Hughes' *The Weary Blues* three years away, though both of these poets had become known to readers of the Negro magazine *Crisis* while still in their teens, and Hughes at twenty-one, the year of *Cane*'s publication, could already be called a favorite.

The first fiction of the Negro Renaissance required apologies. It was not first-rate. But it was an anticipation of what was to come later. Even so, it followed *Cane* by a year or two, and Eric Walrond's *Tropic Death* did not come for three. Zora Neale Hurston's first novel was published in 1931, eight years after *Cane*. Richard Wright made his bow with *Uncle Tom's Children* in 1938, fifteen years later. *Invisible Man* by Ralph Ellison followed Toomer's *Cane* by just thirty years. James Baldwin was not born when Toomer began to publish.

Waldo Frank's use of "harbinger" as the word for *Cane* becomes both significant and ironic when we recognize the debt most of these individuals owe Toomer. Consciously or unconsciously, one after another they picked up his cue and began making the "more searching" effort to see life *with* the Negro, "through him." *Cane* heralded an awakening of artistic expression by Negroes that brought to light in less than a decade a surprising array of talents, and these in turn made way for others. An equally significant change in the writing about Negroes paralleled this awakening. Strangely, however, *Cane* was not at all the harbinger Frank seemed to imagine. Despite his promise—a promise which must impress anyone who puts this first book beside the early writings of either Faulkner or Hemingway, Toomer's contemporaries—Jean Toomer rejected his prospects and turned his back on greatness.

The book by which we remember this writer is as hard to classify as its author. At first glance it appears to consist of assorted sketches, stories and a novelette interspersed with poems. Some of the prose is poetic, and often Toomer slips from one form into the other almost imperceptibly. The novelette is constructed like a play.

His characters, always evoked with effortless strength, are as recognizable as they are unexpected in the fiction of that period. Fern is a "creamy brown" beauty so complicated men take her "but get no joy from it." Becky is a white outcast beside a Georgia road who bears two Negro children. Laymon, a preacher-teacher in the same area, "knows more than would be good for anyone other than a silent man." The name character in the novelette *Kabnis* is a languishing idealist finally redeemed from cynicism and dissipation by the discovery of underlying strength in his people.

It doesn't take long to discover that *Cane* is not without design, however. A world of black peasantry in Georgia appears in the first section. The scene changes to the Negro community of Washington, D.C., in the second. Rural Georgia comes up again in the third. Changes in the concerns of Toomer's folk are noted as the setting moves from the Georgia pike to the bustling Negro section in the nation's capital. The change in the level of awareness that the author discloses is more subtle, but it is clearly discernible when he returns to the Georgia background.

A young poet-observer moves through the book. Drugged by beauty "perfect as dusk when the sun goes down," lifted and swayed by folk song, arrested by eyes that "desired nothing that *you* could give," silenced by "corn leaves swaying, rusty with talk," he recognized that "the Dixie Pike has grown from a goat path in Africa." A native richness is here, he concluded, and the poet embraces it with the passion of love.

This was the sensual power most critics noticed and most readers remembered about *Cane.* It was the basis for Alfred Kreymborg's remark in *Our Singing Strength* that "Jean Toomer

is *one* of the finest artists among the dark people, if not *the* finest."
The reviewer for the New York *Herald Tribune* had the rich
imagery of *Cane* in mind when he said, "Here are the high brown
and black and half-caste colored folk of the cane fields, the gin
hovel and the brothel realized with a sure touch of artistry." But
there remained much in the book that he could not understand or
appreciate. Speaking of Toomer's "sometimes rather strident reactions to the Negro," he added that "at moments his outbursts of
emotion approach the inarticulately maudlin," though he had to
admit that *Cane* represented "a distinct achievement wholly unlike anything of this sort done before."

Others found "obscurity" and "mysticism" in the novelette
which comprises the last third of the book. This is not surprising,
for in Toomer's expressed creed "A symbol is as useful to the spirit
as a tool is to the hand," and his fiction is full of them. Add to
puzzling symbols an itch to find "new ways of writing" that led
him to bold experimentation and one may begin to see why Toomer
baffled as he pleased readers interested in writing by or about
Negroes in the early Twenties.

Kreymborg spoke of Toomer as "a philosopher and a psychologist by temperament" and went on to say that "the Washington
writer is now fascinated by the larger, rather than the parochial
interest of the human race, and should some day compose a book
in the grand manner."

Of course, Toomer didn't, or at least he has not published one
up to now, and to this extent Kreymborg has failed as a prophet,
but his reference to Toomer as philosopher and psychologist was
certainly on the mark, and his rather large estimate of this writer's
capacities was significant, considering its date. The "new criticism," as we have come to recognize it, had scarcely been heard
from then, and apparently it has still not discovered Toomer, but
the chances are it may yet find him challenging. He would have
comforted them, I am almost sorry to say, incarnating, as he does,
some of their favorite attitudes. But at the same time, he could
have served as a healthy corrective for others. Whether or not he
would prove less complex or less rewarding than Gertrude Stein or
James Joyce, for example, remains to be determined.

Saunders Redding gave *Cane* a close reading fifteen years after
its publication and saw it as an unfinished experiment, "the conclusion to which we are fearful of never knowing, for since 1923
Toomer has published practically nothing." He meant, one as-
sumes, that Toomer had published little poetry or fiction, or any-

thing else that seemed closely related to *Cane* or to *Cane*'s author. Toomer had published provocative articles here and there as well as a small book of definitions and aphorisms during that time, and since then he has allowed two of his lectures to be published semi-privately. But Redding must be included in the small group who recognized a problem in *Cane* that has yet to be explained.

To him Toomer was a young writer "fresh from the South," who found a paramount importance in establishing "racial kinship" with Negroes in order to treat them artistically. He was impressed by Toomer's "unashamed and unrestrained" love for the race and for the soil and setting that nourished it. He saw a relationship between the writer's "hot, colorful, primitive" moods and the "naïve hysteria of the spirituals," which he held in contrast to "the sophistic savagery of jazz and the blues." *Cane*, he concluded, "was a lesson in emotional release and freedom."

Chapters about Toomer were included in Paul Rosenfeld's *Men Seen* in 1925 and in Gorham B. Munson's *Destinations* in 1928, and elsewhere there are indications that Toomer continued to write and to experiment for at least a decade after the publication of *Cane*. Long stories by him appeared in the second and third volumes of the *American Caravan*. A thoughtful essay on "Race Problems and Modern Society" became part of a volume devoted to *Problems of Civilization* in Baker Brownell's series on "Man and His World." Seven years later, in the *New Caravan* of 1936, Toomer presented similar ideas in the long poem "Blue Meridian." Meanwhile, contributing a chapter to the book *America & Alfred Stieglitz* in 1934, Toomer was explicit about his own writing as well as several other matters.

The rumor that Toomer had crossed the color line began circulating when his name stopped appearing in print. But a reasonable effort to find out what it was Toomer was trying to say to us subsequently makes it hard to accept "passing" as the skeleton key to the Jean Toomer mystery. He seemed too concerned with truth to masquerade. One wants to believe that Toomer's mind came at last to reject the myth of race as it is fostered in our culture. A man of fair complexion, indistinguishable from the majority of white Americans, he had always had a free choice as to where he would take his place in a color-caste scheme. Having wandered extensively and worked at odd jobs in a variety of cities before he began contributing to little magazines, as he has stated, he could scarcely have escaped being taken at face value by strangers who had no way of knowing that the youth, who looked like

Hollywood's conception of an Ivy League basketball star, but who spoke so beautifully, whose very presence was such an influence upon them, was not only a product of the Negro community but a grandson of the man whom the *Dictionary of American Biography* describes as "the typical Negro politician of the Reconstruction."

Men of this kind, such as Walter White of the NAACP or Adam Clayton Powell of the U.S. Congress, sometimes called voluntary Negroes when they elect to remain in the fold, so to speak, have in other circumstances been discovered in strange places in our society—in neo-fascist organizations in the United States, among big city bosses, on movie screens, in the student body at "Ole Miss"—but seldom if ever before in an organization working "for understanding between people." Yet Jean Toomer's first publication, following the rumors and the silence, was "An Interpretation of Friends Worship," published by the Committee on Religious Education of Friends General Conference, 1515 Cherry Street, Philadelphia, 1947. It was followed two years later by a pamphlet, "The Flavor of Man." The writing is eloquent with commitment. It reflects unhurried reading and contemplation, as was also true of his piece on "Race Problems and Modern Society." Toomer did not fail to remind his readers that certain racial attitudes could not be condoned. He certainly did not speak as a Negro bent on escaping secretly into white society. Jean Toomer, who, like his high-spirited grandfather, had exuberantly published his pride in his Negro heritage, appears to have reached a point in his thinking at which categories of this kind tend to clutter rather than classify. The stand he appears to have taken at first involved nothing more clandestine than the closing of a book or the changing of a subject.

Yet he is on record as having denied later that he was a Negro. That is a story in itself. Nevertheless, at that point, it seems, Jean Toomer stepped out of American letters. Despite the richness of his thought, his gift of expression, he ceased to be a writer and, as I have suggested, turned his back on greatness. His choice, whatever else may be said about it, reflects the human sacrifices in the field of the arts exacted by the racial myth on which so much writing in the United States is based. While he may have escaped its structures and inconveniences in his personal life, he did not get away from the racial problem in any real sense. His dilemmas and frustrations as a writer are equally the dilemmas and frustrations of the Negro writers who have since emerged. The fact that most of them have not been provided with his invisible cloak makes little difference. He is their representative man. He stands as their prototype.

What, then, ordinarily happened to the Negro writer of Toomer's time in America after his first phase, after he had been published and taken his first steps? Encouraged by reviewers, assured that his talent was genuine, that he was not *just* a Negro writer but an American writer who happened to be a Negro, that his first book had broken new ground and that his next would be awaited with keen interest unrelated to any exotic qualities he may have shown but simply as arresting art, he was readily convinced. The "American writer" tag was especially appealing. It stuck in his mind, and when he got the bad news from the sales department, he coupled it with remarks he had heard from his publishers about a certain "resistance" in bookstores to books about "the problem." Obviously the solution for him, as an American writer, was not to write narrowly about Negroes but broadly about people.

So sooner or later he did it: a novel not intended to depict Negro life. The results may be examined: Paul Laurence Dunbar's *The Love of Landry*, Richard Wright's *Savage Holiday*, Chester B. Himes' *Cast the First Stone*, Ann Petry's *Country Place*, Zora Neale Hurston's *Seraph on the Suwanee*, James Baldwin's *Giovanni's Room*, along with Jean Toomer's *York Beach*. While the implication that books about whites are about people while those about Negroes are *not* should have provoked laughter, the young Negro writer was too excited to catch it. The discovery which followed was that the bookstore "resistance" was not removed by this switch. Moreover, he found to his dismay that friendly reviewers had in most instances become cool. In any case, none of these writers seemed sufficiently encouraged by the results to continue in the same direction. Whatever it was that blocked the Negro writer of fiction, that denied him the kind of acceptance accorded the Negro maker of music, for example, was clearly not just the color of his characters.

Southern white novelists from T. S. Stribling to Julia Peterkin to DuBose Heyward to William Faulkner to Robert Penn Warren had thronged their novels with Negroes of all descriptions without appearing to meet reader resistance or critical coolness. So now it could be seen that the crucial issue was not the choice of subject but the author's attitude toward it. With this knowledge the young Negro writers pondered and then made their decisions. Dunbar chose drink. Wright and Himes went to Paris to think it over, as did James Baldwin, at first. Toomer disappeared into Bucks County, Pennsylvania. Frank Yerby, on the basis of a short story in *Harper's Magazine* and a manuscript novel that went the rounds without finding a publisher, took the position that "an unpublished writer, or even one published but unread, is no writer at all." He chose "entertainment" over "literature," and worked his way out of the segregated area of letters in the costume of a riverboat gambler. His book *The Foxes of Harrow* about the Mississippi riverboat gambler became the first successful non-Negro novel by a Negro American writer.

A curious historical irony is suggested. The memoirs of George H. Devol, published in 1887 under the title *Forty Years a Gambler on the Mississippi*, relates the following about a cabin boy called Pinch:

> I raised him and trained him. I took him out of a steamboat barber shop. I instructed him in the mysteries of card-playing, and he was an apt pupil. . . .

Devol recalled with much amusement a night they left New Orleans on the steamer *Doubloon:*

> There was a strong team of us—Tom Brown, Holly Chappell, and the boy Pinch. We sent Pinch and staked him to open a game of chuck-aluck with the Negro passengers on deck, while we opened up monte in the cabin. The run of luck that evening was something grand to behold. I do not think there was a solitary man on the boat that did not drop around in the course of the evening and lose his bundle. When about thirty miles from New Orleans a heavy fog overtook us, and it was our purpose to get off and walk about six miles to Kennersville, where we could take the cars to the city.
>
> Pinchback got our valises together, and a start was made. A drizzling rain was falling, and the darkness was so great that one could not see his hand before his face. Each of us grabbed a valise except Pinch, who carried along the faro tools. The walking was so slippery that we were in the mud about every ten steps, and poor Pinch he groaned under the load that he carried. At last he broke out:
>
> "Tell you what it is, Master Devol, I'll be dumbed if this aint rough on Pinch. Ise going to do better than this toting along old faro tools."
>
> "What's that, Pinch? What you going to do?"
>
> "Ise going to get into that good old Legislature and I'll make Rome howl if I get there."
>
> Of course I thought at the time that this was all bravado and

brag; but the boy was in earnest, and sure enough he got into the Legislature, became Lieutenant Governor, and by the death of the Governor he slipped into the gubernatorial chair, and at last crawled into the United States Senate.

Without necessarily accepting the gambler Devol as an authority on Reconstruction history we may still take his account as substantially factual. P. B. S. Pinchback himself often referred to his career on the river. He was still a prominent public figure when these memoirs were published. He could have denied them had he wished. That Frank Yerby, who became a teacher in a Negro college in Louisiana after his graduation from Fisk University, should center the story of *The Foxes of Harrow* around a Mississippi riverboat gambler is not an odd coincidence. But that Jean Toomer should be the grandson of Pinchback and one of the two people to accompany his body back to New Orleans for burial in 1921 suggests another historical irony.

The behavior pattern known sociologically as "passing for white," then, has its literary equivalent, and the question it raises is whether or not this is proper in the arts. The writer's desire to widen his audience by overcoming what has been called resistance to racial material is certainly understandable, but sooner or later the Negro novelist realizes that what he has encountered, as often critical as popular, is more subtle than that. What annoys some readers of fiction, it seems, is not so much that characters in a book are Negro or white or both as the *attitude of the writer* toward these characters. Does he accept the status quo with respect to the races? If so, any character or racial situation can be taken in stride, not excluding miscegenation. But rejection of traditional status, however reflected, tends to alienate these readers.

On the other hand, the Negro reader has little taste for any art in which the racial attitudes of the past are condoned or taken for granted. Since this is what he has come to expect in the fiction in which he sees himself, he too has developed resistance. His is a wider resistance to the whole world of the contemporary novel. To him literature means poetry, by and large. He knows Phillis Wheatley and Paul Laurence Dunbar far better than he knows any prose writers of the past. James Weldon Johnson and Countee Cullen are familiar and honored names. There is seldom a sermon in a Negro church, a commencement, a banquet, a program in which one of these or a contemporary poet like Hughes or Margaret Walker or Gwendolyn Brooks is not quoted. But the Negro novelists, aside from Richard Wright, possibly, are lumped with the whole questionable lot in the mind of this reader. When he is not offended by the image of himself that modern fiction has projected, he is at least embarrassed.

The Negro writer, like the white writer of the South, is a product of the Southern condition. Whether he wills it or not, he reflects the tensions and cross-purposes of that environment. Just as the myth of the old South weakens under close examination, the myth of literature divorced from what have been called sociological considerations dissolves in a bright light.

The fictional world on which most of us first opened our eyes, where the Negro is concerned, is epitomized by a remark made by a character in William Faulkner's *Sartoris*. "What us niggers want ter be free fer, anyhow?" asks old Uncle Simon. "Ain't we got es many white folks now es we kin suppo't?"

The elusiveness of Jean Toomer in the face of complexities like these can well stand for the elusiveness of Negro writers from Charles W. Chesnutt to Frank Yerby. What Toomer was trying to indicate to us by the course he took still intrigues, but I suspect he realizes by now that there is no further need to *signify*. The secrets are out. As the song says, "There's no hiding place down here."

Darwin T. Turner

The Failure of a Playwright[1]

In 1922 Sherwood Anderson wrote to a twenty-seven-year-old poet and short story writer, "You are the only Negro I've seen who seems really to have consciously the artist's impulse." [2] One might quibble that Mr. Anderson revealed his ignorance of or disdain for Paul Laurence Dunbar and Charles Chesnutt, but his tribute only faintly echoed the praise lavished on Jean Toomer in the early 1920's by Waldo Frank, Gorham Munson, W. S. Braithwaite, Allen Tate, and Robert Littell, literary figures whose pronouncements commanded respect. For the general reader, Toomer's reputation rests upon *Cane* (1923), a collection of stories, sketches, and poems of such high quality that historians of literature by American Negroes mourn his failure to produce more books. Almost unknown, however, is his struggle to succeed as a dramatist. For more than a decade Jean Toomer experimented with dramatic form and technique in order to blend social satire with lyric expression of modern man's quest for spiritual self-realization. It was, as Waldo Frank wrote, an aim so new that it required a new form.[3]

The 1920's were so marked by experimentation in the American theater that pioneering playwrights and set-designers seem to have conspired to revolt against the form, language, and staging of conventional drama, which purported to imitate or represent the actualities of life. But when Toomer completed his first plays in the spring of 1922, the "revolution" was little more than sniper-fire. The Provincetown players had produced Eugene O'Neill's *The Emperor Jones* (1920) and *The Hairy Ape* (1922). Elmer Rice's expressionistic *The Adding Machine* and John Howard Lawson's *Roger Bloomer* would not be produced until 1923. Two to seven years away were other experimental dramas by O'Neill and Lawson, by George Kaufman and Marc Connelly, by John Dos Passos,

---

Reprinted from *CLA Journal,* X (June, 1967), 308–18, by permission of the College Language Association and the author.
[1] This essay is based on research made possible by a study grant from the American Council of Learned Societies.
[2] Letter from Anderson to Toomer, undated, c. 1923. All letters and unpublished manuscripts referred to in this essay are housed in the Jean Toomer Collection at Fisk University, Nashville, Tennessee.
[3] Letter from Frank to Toomer, April 25, 1922.

E. E. Cummings, Sophie Treadwell, and Channing Pollock. Toomer, therefore, did not imitate a literary fad; he was sufficiently far ahead of his time that success would have assured him an important place in the annals of American drama.

Unlike Rice, Kaufman and Connelly, and some of the other dramatists, he did not exploit the novelty of dramatic techniques which had been popularized in other countries. He sought to perfect a technique by which he might most effectively use his artistic talent to objectify mankind's spiritual struggle and to ridicule the society which chains man with false moral standards and false values. Toomer's unique talent, as he later demonstrated in *Cane*, was a lyric impressionism which demanded language more flexible than the patter imitating actual conversations. He needed intensity to express the powerful emotions of his protagonists; but he also needed stylized artificiality to reflect the dullness and superficiality of the guardians of middle-class morals. The emotional impact of the scenes often depends not on the words but on the tone created by the words. Because he was concerned with mankind rather than with private men, he imitated the German Expressionistic playwrights who posited each character for a human type. And he elevated dance from its customary functions of spectacle and mood; literally and symbolically, it is the rhythmic means by which characters release themselves from inhibiting forces. To achieve these effects, he needed the flexibility of nonrepresentational technique and form. His, therefore, was no deliberate rebellion against the dramatic conventions of his time; those forms simply were inadequate to express his intention.

In his first drama, *Natalie Mann* (1922), Toomer argued for the freedom of the young, middle-class Negro women. . . .

He evidenced more faith in a second play, *Kabnis*, which, a companion piece to *Natalie Mann*, had been written before April, 1922. Published in revised form in *Cane*, *Kabnis* negates the possibility that an intellectual Negro can achieve self-realization in the South.

Ralph Kabnis, a Northern Negro who has been teaching in a Southern school, is discharged when his principal sees him intoxicated. Choosing to remain in the South despite the fears which motivate his drinking, he becomes a handyman and an apprentice in a blacksmith shop. Although he has hoped to root himself in that section of the country which he posits for the ancestral soil of his race, he cannot imitate the natives. Uneducated Negroes reject him because they know that he is different. Unlike Principal Hanby, Kabnis cannot compensate for his lost self-respect by abusing less powerful Negroes. Trained to a middle-class respect for education and humiliated to a fear of white Southerners, he cannot pattern after Blacksmith Halsey, who, contemptuous of formal education, enjoys manual labor, and, secure in his self-esteem, loses no dignity when he greets his white customers deferentially. Poetically sensitive and easily shocked, Kabnis cannot imitate Layman, a jackleg preacher, who preserves his own life by mutely observing the abuse, the injustice, and the violence inflicted upon Negroes while he safeguards his income by offering them relief through the fervor of a primitive religion which he knows to be impotent. Insufficiently sensual to control Stella, who has been born of the lust of white men and victimized by the lust of leaders of the Negro community, Kabnis must content himself physically with Cora, whose sensuality is imitative, and spiritually with Carrie K, a youthful, pure, mother-image. Debauched, impotent himself, cognizant of the impotence of education and religion, he awaits inspiration and guidance to come from the message of Father John, an incoherent babbler from the Negro's past. But when Father John finally mumbles something which can be understood, it is merely the banal. "The white people sinned when they made the Bible lie." As the play ends, Kabnis, carrying a bucket of dead coals to his workshop, trudges upward from the basement where Father John is dying in the arms of Carrie K.

The only scintillating ray in this morbid allegory of Negro impotence is Lewis, who, like Nathan Merilh, is both an ectype of Jean Toomer and a Christ-figure. Reared in the North, educated, sensitive but not poetically ineffectual, he can control his actions by will and reason, or can respond naturally to emotional impulse, the life-force, which orders the spiritual and physical union of male with female. Having contracted with himself to remain among his people for a month, he observes them compassionately and communicates satisfactorily with all of them. Sympathetic but emotionally detached, he offers help but is forced to leave when they seek instead the anodynes of drink and sex.

Lacking *Natalie Mann's* lyric language, exciting dances, and satirical social commentary, *Kabnis* has the somber tone of a medieval morality play, written in the style of twentieth-century Expressionism. For Toomer the play proved a disappointment. For two years he tried unsuccessfully to arrange a staging, but pro-

ducers' reactions can be defined by the rejection by Kenneth Macgowan, one of the most daring experimental producers of his generation:

> It won't do as it stands. The dialogue is good dialogue, the char-
> acters are exceedingly good. The incidents are most of them very
> interesting. But I feel that the play lacks the one thing a play
> can't lack—a general dramatic design.[4]

Unfortunately for Toomer, he and Macgowan preceded the
Theater of the Absurd. Macgowan could not see beyond Eugene
O'Neill, who experimented with plot construction, language, setting, and sound, but who worked within a clearly defined plot
which had both beginning and end. Toomer's efforts anticipated
the dramas of Samuel Beckett and Ionesco. Like *Waiting for
Godot*, *Kabnis* is a spectacle of futility and impotence. Like
Ionesco's *The Chairs*, it suspensefully prepares for a trenchant
summation of life, which will give meaning to the play and to life
itself; but the expected explosion is muted in both plays to the wet-
sack whisper of a banal restatement of the obvious. Judged by the
standards of 1922, *Kabnis* is a pale form of the Expressionism
which had not yet become familiar in America; judged by the
standards of 1966, it is good Theater of the Absurd. . . .

Despite imaginative techniques, occasionally striking character-
izations, and frequently brilliant dialogue, Toomer failed to sell
his nonrepresentational drama to producers of his generation. Ac-
customed to looking for a plot in even the most abstract Expressionistic drama they knew, they were irritated to find only a
lecture by Jean Toomer, masked as Christ or Mephistopheles. At
least two of the plays—*Kabnis* and *The Sacred Factory*—merit,
however, a sympathetic reading by a contemporary producer of off-
Broadway theater. Conditioned by Beckett, Ionesco, Genet, and
Albee to the intellectual excitement of spending a few hours puzzling out the meaning of a play, audiences of the Sixties are sufficiently sophisticated to appreciate Jean Toomer's expression of
the futility and the frustration of man's existence.

---

[4] Letter from Macgowan to Toomer, dated September 22, 1923.

B. White Critics

Jean Toomer

Momentarily the prose of *Cane* is artificially exalted, hooked to the Frankian pitch as to a nail high up in the wall. And night is the soft belly of a pregnant negress, and "her mind" a pink mesh bag filled with baby toes. But quickly the inflations subside. The happy normal swing resumes, the easy rhythm of a strainless human frame.

Not all the narratives intend the quality of legendary song. Certain give the fragmentated moods of the contemporary psychic conflict, and throb with hysterical starts and tearing dissonance. Yet saving the few derailing exaltations, the swing and balance of the limber body walking a road is ever-present. The musical state of soul seems primary in Jean Toomer. The pattern generates the tale. He tunes his fiddle like a tavern minstrel, and out of the little rocking or running design there rises the protagonist, solidifying from rhythm as heroes once solidified from mist: crouched white-woman Becky who had two negro sons; Carma in overalls and strong as any man; Kabnis with his jangling nerves and flooding nostalgic lyricism. The rhythm forms the figures most. The words are but flecks of light gleaming on the surface of bronze.

He has his hand lightly, relaxedly, upon substances. The words transmit the easy sensations. They come warm and fuzzy and rich not with the heat and density of bodies crowded in tenements, but with the level beat of a blood promenaded in resinous forests amid blotches of June sun on needles and cones. It is the "sawdust glow of night" and the "velvet pine-smoke air." "The sun which has been slanting over her shoulder, shoots primitive rockets into her mangrove-gloomed, yellow flower face." He assembles words as a painter negligently rubbing pastels; leaving where he touches warm singing blobs of brown and red.

There are no rings laming this imagination, most the time: and binding it in on his proper person. Toomer's protagonists, symbols

Reprinted from *Men Seen: Twenty-four Modern Authors* (New York: The Dial Press, 1925), pp. 227–33. Copyright © 1925 by The Dial Press.

93

and situations are not of the nature of prearrangements: objects
glued together on a mental plane and revealing through wooden
joints and inner dislocation the artificial synthesis. His creative
power offers to bring this young poet-novelist high in the ranks of
living American letters. Characters and narratives move, and move
in unpremeditated, unpredictable curves. Yet in their sudden
tangential departures and radical developments they remain log-
ical with a logic profounder than the intellect's. Not all the person-
ages and situations of the stories, it is true, are submitted to
extended composition and developed. The majority remain exposed
in a single scene and through a single view. Yet in the nouvelle
Kabnis Toomer has produced an extended composition. The focal
character is moved through several episodes, and with each episode
the scope of the story deepens. Characters and situations are satisfying both as symbol and as fact; and toward the conclusion both
are transposed without violence to a level of reality deeper than
that upon which they were launched. Possibly the upper conscious level of mind alone could have produced the earlier scenes;
they may be semi-autobiographical, and felt with the aid of Sherwood Anderson and *The Portrait of the Artist as a Young Man.*
But not the fantastic scene in the cellar, with its opposition of the
torn differentiating negroids and the figure of the ancient African
slave mumbling in his corner. Some inner substance in the author
moved while writing this tale. He was no longer the same man
who began it, when writing the end. He had stepped on a level of
pure invention.

Toomer's free gift has given him the vision of a parting soul, and
lifted his voice in salutation to the folk-spirit of the negro South.
He comes like a son returned in bare time to take a living full farewell of a dying parent; and all of him loves and wants to commemorate that perishing naïveté, only beautiful one America has
had, before universal ugly sophistication cover it also. Those simple singing people who have joy and have pain, and voice them
frankly, largely, utterly have come to hold for him a great earthly
beauty and tragedy. Their sheer animal litheness and pathos has
become savage and satisfying to his breast:

> A feast of moon and men and barking hounds
> An orgy for some genius of the South
> With blood-hot eyes and cane lipped scented mouth—

He follows the elasticity, resiliency of young rubber, into the brown
belt of Washington: feels it in its conflict with the sophistication

and mechanization of white America; watches it weakened and threatened and torn in the bodies of self-conscious, half-educated people, girls become self-centered and men playing the piano in vaudeville theatres and going dreaming of Walt Whitman under the lamps of Seventh Street. And here he perceives, like new strange harmonies sounding through the subtle dissonances of life, promises of an inner healing for these splintered souls, a new strength, swiftness and singleness of motive. A new soul calls. The negroid poet of the story pulled from his base by the wilfulness of a passionate white girl, half lets his amorous opportunity pass in a proud gesture of balladry. Through the woof of *Kabnis* there go the figures of Lewis and Carrie; and Lewis is a man who has become fearless and self-confident and fine; and Carrie is a girl in whom has persisted flowerlike a beauty of instinct.

But these figures are prophetic not only for men of negro blood. They throw forward much in America; for they are symbols of some future America of which Jean Toomer by virtue of the music in him is a portion. He looks two ways. Through this recognition of the beauty of a doomed simplicity some simplicity, sensuosity, passionateness not of the South or of the past asserts, cries out, comes conscious of itself: some America beyond the newspapers, regimented feelings, edgeless language—timid, uncertain, young— in streaming music nevertheless drawing more imminent.

Both Anderson and Frank have helped rouse the impulse of Toomer. Yet it was the imagists with their perfect precision of feeling that fevered him most for work. Some clarity in himself must have responded to the clearness of these poets. That his definiteness remains as yet less intense than theirs is plain. Perhaps because his gift is warmer and more turbulent, it is also less white and clear. Whatever the cause, the Frankian inflations, and the wobbling of the focus between Kabnis and Lewis in the finale of the novelette, leave the indecision a little plainer than we would have it. Large as is the heralding which comes through him, Toomer remains as yet much of the artist trying out his colors, the writer experimenting with a style. And still, these movements of prose are genuine and new. Again a creative power has arrived for American literature: for fiction, perhaps for criticism; in any case, for prose. Other writers have tried, with less happiness, to handle the material of the South. They have had axes to grind; sadisms to exhaust in whipping up passion for the whites; masochisms to release in waking resentment for the blacks. But Toomer comes to unlimber a soul, and give of its dance and music.

Gorham B. Munson

The Significance of Jean Toomer

There can be no question of Jean Toomer's skill as a literary craftsman. A writer who can combine vowels and liquids to form a cadence like "she was as innocently lovely as a November cotton flower" has a subtle command of word-music. And a writer who can break the boundaries of the sentences, interrupt the placement of a fact with a lyrical cry, and yet hold both his fact and his exclamation to a single welded meaning as in the expression: "A single room held down to earth . . . O fly away to Jesus . . . by a leaning chimney . . . ," is assuredly at home in the language and therefore is assuredly free to experiment and invent. Toomer has found his own speech, now swift and clipped for violent narrative action, now languorous and dragging for specific characterizing purposes, and now lean and sinuous for the exposition of ideas, but always cadenced to accord with an unusually sensitive ear.

It is interesting to know that Toomer, before he began to write, thought of becoming a composer. One might have guessed it from the fact that the early sketches in *Cane* (1923) depend fully as much upon a musical unity as upon a literary unity. *Karintha*, for example, opens with a song, presents a theme, breaks into song, develops the theme, sings again, drops back into prose, and dies away in a song. But in it certain narrative functions—one might mention that lying back of the bald statement, "This interest of the male, who wishes to ripen a growing thing too soon, could mean no good to her"—are left undeveloped. Were it not for the songs, the piece could scarcely exist.

But electing to write, Toomer was too canny to try to carry literature further into music than this. *Cane* is, from one point of view, the record of his search for suitable literary forms. We can see him seeking guidance and in several of the stories, notably *Fern* and *Avey*, it is the hand of Sherwood Anderson that he takes hold. But Anderson leads toward formlessness and Toomer shakes him off for Waldo Frank in such pieces as *Theatre* where the design becomes clear and the parts are held in a vital esthetic union. Finally, he breaks through in a free dramatic form of his own, the

---

Reprinted from *Opportunity*, III (September, 1925), 262–63, by permission of Mrs. Gorham B. Munson.

play *Kabnis* which still awaits production by an American theatre that cries for good native drama and yet lacks the wit to perceive the talent of Toomer.

The form of *Kabnis* is a steep slope downward. In the first scene Ralph Kabnis, a neurotic educated Negro who has returned to Georgia from the North, stands on the top of the slope and delivers a monologue, which reveals his character as that of a frustrated lyricist. In Scene Two he begins to fall in the direction of his weaknesses, in Scene Three there occurs an opportunity to check his descent, but his momentum carries him straight past it, and in the remaining scenes he lands in a cellar of debauchery. The action of the play then is linear, but what Kabnis falls through is a rich milieu composed of a symbolic ancient Negro who has experienced slavery, an honest craft-loving wheelwright, a bourgeois school supervisor, a clear-headed forceful radical black, a couple of prostitutes, a church audience, a minister, and little Carrie K., fresh symbol of a possible future. Toomer's formal achievement is just this: to utilize a milieu and a character, the first as a dense living slope, the second as a swiftly descending point tracing out a line of action upon the first.

It is necessary and important that an artist should be in command of his tools, but if we feel that craftsmanship is only a means to an end, we must proceed to inquire what end Toomer's skill was designed to suit.

Cane is the projection of a vivid personality. What the fundamental motives were that impelled this projection we cannot say, but we can pick out a few probably subsidiary motives that will perhaps indicate Toomer's status at the moment he completed *Cane*. Clearly, he desired to make contact with his hereditary roots in the Southland. One of the poems in *Cane* is an unmistakable recognition of this desire.

> "O land and soil, red soil and sweet-gum tree,
> So scant of grass, so profligate of pines,
> Now just before an epoch's sun declines
> Thy son, in time, I have returned to thee,
> Thy son, I have in time returned to thee."

From this one infers a preceding period of shifting and drifting without settled harborage. Weary of homeless waters, he turns back to the ancestral soil, opens himself to its folk-art and its folk-ways, tries to find his roots, his origins. It is a step toward the definition of himself.

What can we add to this purpose? We can say that Toomer makes a very full response to life, a response that is both robust and sensitive, and we can say, to use the conventional phrase, that he "accepts life." It is plain that he has strong instincts, welling and deep and delicate emotions, and a discriminating and analytical intellect (more fully revealed in his critical work); and these are all keenly aware of life. This life that floods in upon his equipment Toomer finds to be potent and sweet, colorful and singing, interesting and puzzling, pathetic and worthy of respect; he is able to accept it,—perhaps because his survey of it shows it to be beautiful and mysterious. As any rate, the only fully adumbrated attitude in *Cane* is that of the spectatorial artist. But that raises the question, under what circumstances can the artist be a spectator?

To be a spectator one must have a firm and fixed point of vantage. Where can such a point be found today? Our social framework is admittedly unsettled, but it is less generally perceived that culturally we are being blown into chaos. Our heritage came from Judea, Greece and Rome, and to that heritage we have added science. Today, it needs but a glance at the vitality of the early Christians and at the legalism and stupor of the modern church to realize that something basic and essential has passed away from Christianity. From the testimony of the humanists themselves we are entitled to conclude that humanism is in decay. And science, upon which the nineteenth century depended, has turned to inner conflict, uncertainty and groping. In short, the Occidental world now has no one body of common experience, no ancestral faith, no *concensus omnium bonorum*, no principle of unification, put it how you will, to which men everywhere may make appeal and upon which the spectatorial artist might situate himself. The great movement of the last few centuries has been romanticism which has glorified personal uniqueness and universal flux and has driven us all away from any possible center of human experience. Born into such circumstances, what is the artist to do? He must choose to work either toward integration or toward disintegration.

Nietzsche, it should be recalled, looked upon artists as casters of glamor over progression and retrogression alike. That is, by virtue of their magic they could glorify either, they could be their saviors or betrayers. An artist who does not care where the lure and grace that he sheds over the objects led his entranced followers naturally will not inquire very deeply into his purpose for creation. He creates beauty and lets truth and goodness go hang. But an artist who feels that his gifts entail a grave responsibility, who wishes to fight on the side of life abundant rather than for life deficient, must pause and seek the answers to certain questions. What is the function of man? What are the potentials of man and what may he become? What is experience and what is knowledge? What is the world?

The significance of Jean Toomer lies in his strenuous attempt to answer these questions. Shortly after writing *Cane*, he formed two convictions. One was that the modern world is a veritable chaos and the other was that in a disrupted age the first duty of the artist is to unify himself. Having achieved personal wholeness, then perhaps he would possess an attitude that would not be merely a reaction to the circumstances of modernity, merely a reflection of the life about him, but would be an attitude that could act upon modernity, dissolve away the remainder of an old slope of consciousness, and plant the seeds for a new slope.

So he turned to an intensive study of his own psychology. He sifted psychoanalysis for what minute grains of truth it might supply, he underwent the training for "conscious control of the body" prescribed by F. Matthias Alexander, he spent a summer at the Gurdjieff Institute, Fontainebleau, France, where he obtained what he regards as the best method for his quest. We should note that his search is distinguished from that of many other American artists (Sherwood Anderson may be cited as typical) by its positive scientific character. These others work from a disgust or a negation. They cut loose from something they abhor and, unprovided with any method, drift aimlessly in search of a leaven which somewhere, somehow, will heal. Toomer has a method and an aim, and he devoted his whole time and energy to them. In his own words, this is what he is doing: "I am. What I am and what I may become I am trying to find out."

He is a dynamic symbol of what all artists of our time should be doing, if they are to command our trust. He has mastered his craft. Now he seeks a purpose that will convince him that his craft is nobly employed. Obviously, to his search there is no end, but in his search there is bound to occur a fusion of his experience, and it is this fused experience that will give profundity to his later work. His way is not the way of the minor art master, but the way of the major master of art. And that is why his potential literary significance outweighs the actualized literary significance of so many of his contemporaries.

David Littlejohn

Before *Native Son:* The Renaissance and After

The four most discussed Negro poets of the period, Jean Toomer, Countee Cullen, Claude McKay, and Langston Hughes, were all genuine poets of the new dispensation, not mere imitators or verse-makers. Theirs is, really, the first American Negro writing one can judge absolutely, with no necessary reference to its context. They are better than the earlier Negro poets not because they are New Negroes, but because American poetry itself grew up in the 1920's, and they were there. Of the four, even the least worthy is of serious consequence, by comparison with earlier names in our survey. . . .

Jean Toomer's career is still wrapped in foggy mystery: he wrote one esoteric work, difficult to grasp, define, and assess; he was associated with one of the more advanced white modernist cults, and adopted and taught Russian mysticism; and then he suddenly declared himself white, and disappeared.

His book, *Cane* (1923), is composed of fourteen prose pieces, ranging from two- and four-page sketches, to "Kabnis," an eighty-three-page *nouvelle;* and fifteen detached poems set in between.

About half the "stories" have tiny lyric refrains tucked inside them as well.

The prose pieces in the first section of the book are detached vignettes of high female sexuality among the Negro peasants of the Dixie Pike. They are drawn with the new honest artfulness of the Stein-Anderson-Hemingway tradition, so crisp and icily succinct that the characters seem bloodless and ghostly, for all the fury of their indicated lives, all style and tone and suggestion. It is into this section that Toomer's finest poems are set—"Song of the Son," "Georgia Dusk," "Portrait in Georgia"—poems which reveal a great deal about his viewpoint and method. They are the most freely experimental Negro poems of the generation, far freer even than Langston Hughes' games with the rhythms of jazz and conversation. They view Southern Negro life with a chilling objectivity ("so objective he might not be a Negro," an early critic prophetically observed). Common things are seen as if through a strangely neurotic vision, transformed into his own kind of nightmare.

> Hair—braided chestnut, coiled like a lyncher's rope,
> Eyes—fagots,
> Lips—old scars, or the first red blisters,
> Breath—the last sweet scent of cane,
> And her slim body, white as the ash of black flesh after flame.

In "Song of the Son" he tries to identify himself with the Georgia soil, but the very effort makes clear his distant view; the view of a sophisticated surrealist among an alien peasantry, a peasantry he transforms into something duskily primeval.

> O Negro slaves, dark purple ripened plums,
> Squeezed, and bursting in the pine-wood air,
> Passing, before they stripped the old tree bare
> One plum was saved for me, one seed becomes
>
> An everlasting song, a singing tree,
> Caroling softly souls of slavery,
> What they were, and what they are to me,
> Caroling softly souls of slavery.

The prose pieces of the second section support this view, though now his bony surrealist's objectivity is transferred to Northern urban Negroes. In the two key stories, "Box Seat" and "Bona and Paul," he runs hot wires of anti-realism beneath a surface of realistic events, somewhat in the manner of Malcolm Lowry or John Hawkes, to imply a strange neurotic derangement in his characters. It is primarily a matter of imagery:

> Through the cement floor her strong roots sink down. They spread under the asphalt streets. Dreaming, the streets roll over on their bellies, and suck their glossy health from them. Her strong roots sink down and spread under the river and disappear in blood-lines that waver south. Her roots shoot down. Dan's hands follow them. Roots throb. . . .

The long story "Kabnis" that makes up the third part is crafted of nervous images and a strong sense of interior pain. The underground cellar symbolism is disturbing, as is, again, the utter objectivity of the narration. But the story drifts off into a hazy poetic incoherence, and—like most of the book, finally—is too insubstantial to be remembered. For all that, the book should really be allowed to come back into print.

Frank Durham

Jean Toomer's Vision
of the Southern Negro

When Jean Toomer's strange book *Cane* appeared in 1923, the few who read it were treated to a vision of the Southern Negro, a vision seen, I believe, through bifocals, or even trifocals. But most of the critics then and since have peered at this vision through only one or at most two of Toomer's lenses. The result has been that Toomer's picture of the Southern Negro has been only partially understood and partially interpreted.

Printed by permission of the editors of *The Southern Humanities Review,* in which journal the essay will appear as part of a forthcoming symposium on Southern writers.
Quotations from *Cane* by Jean Toomer, copyright (R) 1951 by Jean Toomer, reprinted by permission of the Liveright Publishing Corporation, New York.

The most obvious response to *Cane* was bewilderment. It was a book of sketches, poems, poetic prose, a short story or two, and something that has been called everything from a novella to a play. Its first section dealt with six women, one of them white, and with a triangular black-and-white love story, all with their setting in rural Georgia and all having a prose style suggesting poetry when it did not soar off into actual verse. Then came a group of sketches, poems, and stories set in Washington and Chicago with their emphasis on the Negro's fading vitality in the urban environment, even as his roots stretched down through the pavements to the Southern soil. Here a white-and-black love story ended, not as in the first section, in bloodshed and a lynching, but in a kind of futile fading away. Finally, there was "Kabnis," a longish piece, again set in rural Georgia, shifting between fairly straight fictional narrative with poetic and symbolic overtones and a kind of dramatic dialogue that led its author to seek its production on a stage. But there was obviously an allegorical intent, though exactly what it was left critics murmuring "obscure," "puzzled," and "a hazy incoherence."

The most frequently cited element in Toomer's vision of the Southern Negro was described in a lecture by Dr. Mabel M. Dillard. She said that in 1923 Toomer was writing what today in black literature is called "soul." In a way that no author, black or white, had done before, he captured and embodied in *Cane* the quintessential nature of the rural Southern Negro. And, for the most part, his background enabled him to do so with an ambivalence not shared by other writers. Reared and educated in the North, he made a pilgrimage to Georgia to discover his roots, his ancestral heritage. Thus he was able to project himself inside the Negro even as he remained in part the outside observer and the conscious artist. Writing in 1939 Saunders Redding said of Toomer:

> . . . he held nothing so important to the artistic treatment of Negroes as racial kinship with them. Unashamed and unrestrained, Jean Toomer loved the race and the soil that sustained it. His moods are hot, colorful, primitive, but more akin to the naive hysteria of the spirituals than to the sophisticated savagery of jazz and the blues. *Cane* was a lesson in emotional release and freedom. Through all its prose and poetry gushes a subjective tide of love.[1]

---

[1] *To Make a Poet Black* (Chapel Hill: University of North Carolina Press, 1939), p. 104.

Toomer himself, writing in 1923 of his attempted fusion of the white and the Negro elements inside himself, said:

> Within the last two or three years, however, my growing need for artistic expression has pulled me deeper and deeper into the Negro group. And as my powers of receptivity increased, I found myself loving it in a way that I could never love the other. It has stimulated and fertilized whatever creative talents I may contain within me.[2]

Later, reporting on his stay in rural Georgia, he wrote:

> There, for the first time, I really saw the Negro, not as a pseudo-urbanized and vulgarized, a semi-Americanized product, but the Negro peasant, strong with the tang of fields and the soil. It was there that I first heard folk-songs rolling up the valley at twilight, heard them as spontaneous with gold, and tints of an eternal purple. Love? They gave birth to a whole new life.[3]

In Georgia, then, Jean Toomer found his ancestral roots in the rural Negro. What he found, as he depicts it in the first section of *Cane*, was a people characterized by a tremendous vitality, a vitality and a liberation of emotion taking their sustenance from the soil, the hot, steamy, red Georgia earth, fertile and lush and almost tropical. As this earth nourished the corn and the cane, so it endowed the Negroes living close to it with a rare, untrammeled élan alien to the white man with his materialism, his unnatural Christian ethic, and his increasing urge to move into towns and cities where both his body and his spirit are "cabin'd, cribb'd, confined." Among the Georgia Negroes Toomer saw this heritage stretching far back, beyond the red Georgia earth and the hot Georgia sun. For, he noted, "The Dixie Pike has grown from a goat path in Africa." In his awareness that the Negro's difference from the white man lies in his being the heir of two cultures simultaneously, the American and the African, Toomer foreshadows the writers of the Harlem School, one of whose basic premises was the advantages the Negro enjoyed because of his double inheritance.

---

[2] Quoted by Mark Schorer, ed., *The Literature of America: The Twentieth Century.* New York: McGraw-Hill Book Co., 1970, p. 528.

[3] "Outline of Autobiography," quoted by Mabel Mayle Dillard in "Jean Toomer: Herald of the Negro Renaissance," unpublished Ph.D. dissertation, Ohio University, 1967, p. 22.

But let us hear the author speak for himself. In "Song of the Son" he synthesizes his vision of the rural Georgia Negro:

> O land and soil, red soil and sweet-gum tree,
> So scant of grass, so profligate of pines,
> Now just before an epoch's sun declines
> Thy son, in time, I have returned to thee,
> Thy son, I have in time returned to thee.
>
> In time, for though the sun is setting on
> A song-lit race of slaves, it has not set;
> Though late, O soil, it is not too late yet
> To catch thy plaintive soul, leaving, soon gone,
> Leaving, to catch thy plaintive soul soon gone.
>
> O Negro slaves, dark purple ripened plums,
> Squeezed, and bursting in the pinewood air,
> Passing, before they stripped the old tree bare
> One plum was saved for me, one seed becomes
>
> An everlasting song, a singing tree,
> Caroling softly souls of slavery,
> What they were, and what they are to me,
> Caroling softly souls of slavery.

Again, in "Georgia Dusk" we have a further development of his image of the Negro:

> A feast of moon and men and barking hounds,
>   An orgy for some genius of the South
>   With blood-hot eyes and cane-lipped scented mouth
> Surprised in making folk-songs from soul sounds.
> . . . .
>
> Meanwhile, the men, with vestiges of pomp,
>   Race memories of king and caravan,
>   High-priests, an ostrich, and a juju-man,
> Go singing through the footpaths of the swamp.
>
> Their voices rise . . the pine trees are guitars,
>   Strumming, pine-needles fall like sheets of rain . .
>   Their voices rise . . the chorus of the cane
> Is caroling a vesper to the stars . .
>
> O singers, resinous and soft your songs
>   Above the sacred whisper of the pines,
>   Give virgin lips to cornfield concubines,
> Bring dreams of Christ to dusky cane-lipped throngs.

Here Toomer stresses the life-giving, freedom-inspiring link with the soil, the simultaneously degrading and exalting (through a kind of purgation) experience of slavery and oppression, the innate gift of song, racial memories reaching back to tribal Africa, a sexuality characterized by both fleshly joys and a childlike innocence, and, finally, the strange, emotional amalgam of paganism and the white man's religion. He emphasizes the Negro's increasing loss of these wholly desirable traits, their corruption by the encroaching of the white man's values and the white man's bigotry.

In his portraits of Negro women there is displayed the close association of their beauty and spirit with the soil and the sun and their primal roots. Karintha "carries beauty, perfect as dusk when the sun goes down"; as a child, "she was as innocently lovely as a November cotton flower," and "the soul of her was a growing thing ripened too soon." Carma, "strong as any man," drives a mule-drawn wagon:

> Nigger woman driving a Georgia chariot down an old dusty road. . . .
> From far away, a sad strong song. Pungent and composite, the smell
> of farmyards is the fragrance of the woman. She does not sing; her
> body is a song. She is in the forest, dancing. Torches flare . . juju
> men, greegree, witch-doctors . . torches go out. . . The Dixie Pike
> has grown from a goat path in Africa.

There is Fern: "Like her face, the whole countryside seemed to flow into her eyes. Flowed into them with the soft listless cadence of Georgia's South." And Esther, with "her high-cheek-boned chalk-white face," confuses sexuality with religious fervor in her visions of King Barlo, the lusty Negro evangelist; for her well-to-do background and her mixed blood inhibit her natural impulses. Seeing Barlo, she wishes that she was "sharp, sporty, with get-up about her. . . . She mustn't wish. Wishes only make you restless." At twenty-seven, trying to make her fantasies true, she confronts Barlo, ready to yield herself, but he is drunk, with coarse men and coarser women who sneer at her for being a "dictie nigger," educated and giving herself airs. She is repelled. "Barlo seems hideous." To conceive a child, even a new saviour, with him "must be a mighty sin." In "Blood Burning Moon," Bob Stone, a white boy, loves Louisa, a black girl, and his impulse to assert the old *droit de seigneur* of his planter class vanishes when he is honest with himself:

> Was there something about niggers that you couldnt know? Listen-
> ing to them at church didnt tell you anything. Looking at them

didnt tell you anything—unless it was gossip, unless they wanted
to talk.

Then he thinks of Louisa and the dangers his affair with her
involves:

She was worth it. Beautiful nigger gal. Why nigger? Why not, just
gal? No, it was because she was nigger that he went to her. Sweet
. . . The scent of boiling cane came to him.

In the second section of *Cane* Toomer moves his setting to Washington and Chicago. Here, while continuing his portrait of the
primitivism and the vitality of the Negro, he emphasizes the rapid
repression and distortion of their traits by the materialism and
acquisitiveness of city life, by the growing caste-snobbery of the
educated Negro in regard to those less so, and by a kind of lostness
which the educated, sensitive Negro experiences—as if he were held
suspended between two worlds, one dying and the other thus far
unattainable.

In "Seventh Street" the Negro district is "A crude-boned, soft-
skinned wedge of nigger life breathing its loafer air, jazz songs and
love, thrusting unconscious rhythms, black reddish blood into the
white and whitewashed wood of Washington." In "Rhobert," the
protagonist "wears a house, like a monstrous diver's helmet on his
head." In "Avey" the title character is a black girl, who rejects the
opportunities for further education and advancement and sinks
into indifference and prostitution. Her innate impulses, her primal
vitality and fertility are distorted by the city. Her would-be lover,
an ambitious black boy, eager for education and getting ahead, fails
her, even as he is really failing himself. Misunderstanding her
need, he says, "There was no excuse for a healthy girl taking life
so easy. Hell! she was no better than a cow. I was certain that she
was a cow when I felt an udder in a Wisconsin stock-judging class."
In fact, he is as lost as she. In "Theater" a "dictie" Negro is drawn
into sexual fantasies involving Dorris, a sensual and natural chorus
girl, but the newly found caste-snobbery blocks the fulfillment of
their desires. John, watching her dance, says, "Dictie, educated;
stuck-up; show-girl. Yep. Her suspicion would be stronger than her
passion. It wouldnt work." And Dorris, fearing his condescension,
thinks: "Aint I as good as him? Couldnt I have got an education if
I'd wanted one? Dont I know respectable folks . . . ?" The new inhibitions quench the ancient, basic, natural spirit of the race. In

"Box Seat" Muriel, the prudish black schoolteacher, rebuffs Dan, a messianic figure, who is drawn by "her animalism" which he wrongly thinks is "still unconquered by zoo-restrictions and keeper-taboos." At the theatre he sits next to

> . . . a portly Negress whose huge rolls of flesh meet about the bones of seat-arms. A soil-soaked fragrance comes from her. Through the cement floor her strong roots sink down. They spread under the asphalt streets. Dreaming, the streets roll over on their bellies, and suck their glossy health from them. Her strong roots sink down and spread under the river and disappear in blood-lines that waver south. Her roots shoot down.

A major element in Toomer's portrayal of the Negro is sexuality, used symbolically in an almost Lawrentian manner. His women are all portrayed in sexual terms. They give of themselves freely, naturally, and those yet uncorrupted joy in the sexual act as a kind of extension of their link with the fertile earth. The black critic W. E. B. DuBois in 1924 called Toomer the "writer who first dared to emancipate the colored world from the conventions of sex. . . . the first of our writers to hurl his pen across the very face of our sex conventionality." [4] To the rural Negro, as Toomer shows him, sex is natural, unashamed, sometimes casual, sometimes intense—but touched by the white man's mores it becomes indifferent, distorted, shameful.

The most frequently cited facet of Toomer's vision of the rural Southern Negro, then—the one seen through the most-used lens—is that showing the Negro as an admirable, primitive, intensely human being—liberated by his kinship with the earth, uninhibited, free, responsive to the soil and the sun, mingling the glories of two cultures, and expressing his soul in native wisdom, in the joyful and sad songs of work and love and religion. Here in 1923 Toomer was, as I have said, anticipating the Harlem School in its stress on the Negro's "Negritude," his soul as something desirable and valuable. Too, he was consciously using the Negro as a subject for art—the new verbal art of Joyce and Sherwood Anderson and even Waldo Frank; but he was also employing the Negro as a subject for art in the way that DuBose Heyward was already tentatively doing in his poetry and was two years later to develop more fully in his novel *Porgy*—the colorful dynamism of the Negro, his innate sense of rhythm, his tragedy, and his laughter. There is a similarity, too,

---

[4] "The Younger Literary Movement," *Crisis,* XXVII (Feb., 1924), 161.

I think, to what Julia Peterkin had begun two years earlier in her short stories and was to elaborate in her novels—writing of the black man from the *inside* in a way that Heyward never did. Like Julia Peterkin, and with considerably more reason, Jean Toomer thought and felt black.

There are other facets of Toomer's vision, but the one most generally ignored or denied entirely is his subtly presented protest at, not only the diminution of the Negro soul by its contacts with white society, but, more relevant to today, the oppression and brutality which the Negro must endure as a result of white fear, bigotry, injustice, and violence.

But let us see what critics, white and black, have said on this subject. Waldo Frank, in his "Foreword" to the 1923 edition of *Cane,* wrote:

> For Toomer, the Southland is not a problem to be solved; it is a field of loveliness to be sung: the Georgia Negro is not a downtrodden soul to be uplifted; he is material for gorgeous painting: the segregated self-conscious brown belt of Washington is not a topic to be discussed and exposed; it is a subject of beauty and of drama, worthy of creation in literary form.[5]

And Eugene Holmes, a black critic, in 1932 praised Toomer by saying:

> At first, critics could not understand that a Negro could write poetry that did not reek with rebellion and propaganda. Toomer wrote as a poet, never as an apologist.

Comparing *Cane* to "the turbulent and rebellious poetry of the [Claude] McKay of that time," he found Toomer's work "a breath of sweet, cool air." [6] Robert Littell maintained that here was not "the South of lynchings and hatreds, of the bitter, rebellious young Negro, and of his emigration to the North." [7] Finally, Hugh M. Gloster wrote: "In this book a colored writer, for possibly the first time in American Negro fiction, handles inflammatory interracial themes without abandonment of the artist's point of view." [8]

It is undeniable that first and foremost Jean Toomer was the

---

5 *Cane.* New York: Boni & Liveright, 1923, pp. viii–ix.
6 "Jean Toomer: Apostle of Beauty," *Opportunity,* X (Aug., 1932), 252.
7 *"Cane,"* *New Republic,* XXXVII (Dec. 26, 1923), 126.
8 *Negro Voices in American Fiction.* Chapel Hill: University of North Carolina, 1948, p. 128.

artist, the poet. But there is no law prohibiting the artist and poet from holding and expressing through his work pronounced opinions. Often the most effective persuasive writing is that which, on the surface at any rate, seems least intended to persuade. It is my belief that, consciously or unconsciously, Jean Toomer presents as a constant element in his picture of the Negro an anger at the injustice, bigotry, and cruelty to which the Negro was subjected. Again and again he portrays examples of this oppression and of its effects on the Negro soul.

In "Becky," one of the six sketches of women, Toomer tells of a poor-white woman who has two Negro children. Having violated the codes of both races, Becky is, on the surface, totally ignored; but, moved by guilt, members of both races secretly build her a cabin and feed her, pretending that she is dead. Her two sons grow up.

> They drifted around from job to job. We, who had cast out their mother because of them, could we take them in? They answered black and white folks by shooting up two men and leaving town. "Godam the white folks; godam the niggers," they shouted as they left town.

Becky's cabin falls in on her. The Negro preacher throws a Bible on the wreckage:

> She's dead; they've gone away. The pines whisper to Jesus. The Bible flaps its leaves with an aimless rustle on her mound.

In "Blood-Burning Moon," Louisa, the black girl, is loved by a white boy and a black boy. When her black lover knifes the white boy, Toomer gives a vivid, moving description of the lynching—artistically done, yes, but with an impact that goes beyond art or rather extends art into a violent protest against injustice and violence:

> Shotguns, revolvers, rope, kerosene, torches. Two high-powered cars with glaring searchlights. They came together. . . . The moving body of their silence preceded them over the crest of the hill into factory town. It flattened the Negroes beneath it. . . . Tom knew that they were coming. He couldnt move. . . . Taut humming. No words. . . . . Kerosene poured on the rotting floor boards. Tom bound to the stake . . . Now Tom could be seen within the flames. Only his head, erect, lean, like a blackened stone. Stench of burning flesh

> soaked the air. Tom's eyes popped. His head settled down. The
> mob yelled. Its yell echoed against the skeleton stone walls and
> sounded like a hundred yells. Like a hundred mobs yelling.

Though individualized, this is not an isolated case, Toomer is saying. The echo of the mob's yell "sounded like a hundred yells. Like
a hundred mobs yelling."

His treatment of the educated, sensitive, poetic observer in the
book is also an example of the Negro's plight. He is Jean Toomer,
whether he is named Kabnis or remains nameless or appears in
other fictional guises. In one sense *Cane* is a protest against the
destruction and degradation, almost the spiritual castration, of the
educated Negro in the America of the 1920's. Making a pilgrimage
from the North to find his ancestral roots, he finds them, but also
finds that he can no longer establish a sense of their belonging to
him. His white man's culture has, if one may mix a metaphor,
severed the umbilical cord. Furthermore, the Negroes who still
share in this heritage reject him too, for he is no longer of them, he
now has acquired the aura of whiteness.

> Kabnis, a promise of a soil-soaked beauty; uprooted, thinning out.
> Suspended a few feet above the soil whose touch would resurrect
> him.

But in the white world, both South and North, he is also an
alien, a stranger. Even as Paul's Negritude attracts the white Bona,
she fears it, and Paul, aware that the discovery of his blackness
may blast his romance and his social ties in white circles, is left
solitary in the empty street, as he is solitary in an empty world.
Rejected by both races, Kabnis ends dissipated and degraded,
failing to find an answer from Father John, the ex-slave, or from
Lewis, the so-called Christ figure, who, remarkably for a Christ,
turns his back on his people because they seek escape from their
hopeless lives in the sins of the flesh.

The story "Kabnis" further elaborates upon what white oppression has done to the Negro by presenting a group of allegorical
characters. Hanby, the school principal, has been driven to being
an Uncle Tom, a hypocritical deferrer to the whites and a cruel op-
pressor of his fellow blacks. Layman, the self-appointed preacher,
sees the injustice around him, but offers his fellows the false com-
forts of an emotional religion in which he scarcely believes. He tells
Kabnis:

Nigger's a nigger down this away, Professor. An only two dividins:
good and bad. An even they aint permanent categories. They sometimes mixes um up when it comes t lynchin. I've seen um do it.

Halsey, the craftsman, has no faith in education for the Negro. He
knows the evils of white tyranny, but to live, he adapts, humbles
himself before the whites, and finds escape in the satisfaction of
working with his hands and the forgetfulness of dissipation. He
says:

An Mr. Kabnis, kindly remember youre in th land of cotton—hell
of a land. The white folks get th boll: th niggers get th stalk. An
dont you dare touch th boll or even look at it. Theyll swing y sho.

The two Negro prostitutes, Stella and Cora, reflect the exploitation
of Negro women by the lust of both white and black men. Stella's
instincts are for love and maternity, but she has been made bitter
and indifferent; Cora has been used physically to the point that
she is almost mindless. Down in Halsey's cellar is the ancient
ex-slave, Father John, seated in a chair on a platform. He is the link
with both slavery and the African past, but the Negroes hide him
as if ashamed. Still, they seek some sort of wisdom from him. But
he is virtually mute. "He is like a bust in black walnut. Gray-
bearded. Gray-haired. Prophetic. Immobile." When he does speak
at last to the by-now-utterly-degraded Kabnis, his words are almost meaningless, about white folks making a lie out of the Bible
—a dull, dead truism without enlightenment.

Two characters in "Kabnis" carry in them a suggestion, but only
a suggestion, of Toomer's tentative solution to the problems of the
Negro. These are Carrie Kate and Lewis. The girl seems to represent the pure, untouched Negro soul, throbbing with the promise
of life and love, a kind of fertility symbol—the ideal lover and the
potential earth mother. She is a food-bringer, nurturing Father
John, the Negro's ancestral past. Lewis is the educated Negro from
the North. "His mouth and eyes suggest purpose guided by an
adequate intelligence. He is what a stronger Kabnis might have
been. . . ." When Lewis and Carrie K. confront each other, Toomer
writes:

Their meeting is a swift sun-burst. Lewis impulsively moves towards her. His mind flashes images of her life in the southern town.

He sees the nascent woman, her flesh already stiffening to carti-
lage, drying to bone. Her spirit-bloom, even now touched sullen,
bitter. Her rich beauty fading. . . He wants to— He stretches forth
his hand to hers. He takes them. They feel like warm cheeks against
his palms. The sun-burst from her eyes floods up and haloes him.
Christ-eyes, his eyes look to her. Fearlessly she loves into them.
And then something happens. Her face blanches. Awkwardly she
draws away. The sin-bogies of respectable southern colored folks
clamor at her: "Look out! Be a *good* girl. A *good* girl. Look out!"
She gropes for her basket that has fallen to the floor. Finds it, and
marches with a rigid gravity to her task of feeding the old man.
Like the glowing white ash of burned paper, Lewis' eyelids, wavering, settle down. He stirs in the direction of the rear window. From
the back yard, mules tethered to odd trees and posts blink dumbly
at him. They too seem burdened with an impotent pain.

Here in this moment of meeting, Toomer possibly offers a solution
to the Negro's subjection by the white—the union of "purpose
guided by an adequate intelligence" and strength with the Negro's
ancient spirit, his life force drawn from the soil and the sun and the
primal past. Of course, he does hint that the solution will be de-
layed until the Negro can cast aside the restrictive, bourgeois
moral-religious taboos of the white man's code. But he does, at
least, hint at a way of battle.

In conclusion, then, Toomer's vision of the rural Southern
Negro is indeed characterized, as many critics agree, by a pioneering glimpse of the vitality of the Negro soul, its beauty, its freedom, its uninhibited expression of the inheritance of two worlds—
the paganism of Africa and the vibrant, fertile soil of the South. It
is true, too, that he shows the corroding effects of white culture on
this soul. But, equally true, though rarely if ever noted, is the fact
that Toomer could not write of the Negro soul without an awareness of more than just the gradual diminution of its exuberance
and power; he could not write of it without portraying the violence
and oppression by the white man and without, consciously or unconsciously, raising his voice in protest, a voice subtler than those
of Walter White, T. S. Stribling, Claude McKay, Langston Hughes,
and others of his own time; a voice certainly subtler than those of
Richard Wright, James Baldwin, LeRoi Jones, Ralph Ellison, and
Eldridge Cleaver. His very subtlety is deceptive, for without shrill-
ness, without overt propaganda, he made his readers share his
sorrow and his burning anger.